CULTURES OF THE WORLD
Chile

mc Marshall Cavendish
Benchmark
New York

PICTURE CREDITS

Cover: © DEGAS Jean-Pierre / age fotostock
Corbis / Click Photos: 19, 28, 29, 31, 55, 56 • Getty Images: 23, 30, 34, 76, 100, 101, 103, 127 • Inmagine: 42, 48, 71, 98, 99, 128, 131 • Lonely Planet Images: 120 • Marshall Cavendish International (Asia): 66, 86, 93 • Lonely Planet Images: 120 • photolibrary: 1, 3, 5, 6, 7, 8, 10, 11, 12, 13, 14, 15, 16, 17, 18, 20, 22, 24, 26, 27, 35, 37, 38, 40, 43, 44, 46, 47, 49, 50, 51, 53, 58, 60, 61, 62, 64, 65, 68, 69, 70, 72, 74, 75, 77, 78, 80, 81, 82, 84, 85, 88, 89, 90, 92, 94, 96, 97, 104, 106, 107, 108, 109, 111, 114, 115, 117, 118, 122, 125, 130 • Reuters: 32,102

PRECEDING PAGE

The undulating landscape of Vegas de Quepiaco in the Antofagasta region of the Atacama Desert, Chile.

Publisher (U.S.): Michelle Bisson
Writers: Jane Kohen Winter and Susan Roraff
Editors: Deborah Grahame-Smith, Mindy Pang
Copyreader: Daphne Hougham
Designers: Nancy Sabato, Benson Tan
Cover picture researcher: Tracey Engel
Picture researcher: Joshua Ang

Marshall Cavendish Benchmark
99 White Plains Road
Tarrytown, NY 10591
Website: www.marshallcavendish.us

© Times Media Private Limited 1990. First Edition.
© Times Media Private Limited 2002. Second Edition.
© Marshall Cavendish International (Asia) Private Limited 2012. Third Edition.
® "Cultures of the World" is a registered trademark of Times Publishing Limited.

Originated and designed by Times Media Private Limited
An imprint of Marshall Cavendish International (Asia) Private Limited
A member of Times Publishing Limited

Marshall Cavendish is a trademark of Times Publishing Limited.

All Internet sites were correct and accurate at the time of printing. All monetary figures in this publication are in U.S. dollars.

Library of Congress Cataloging-in-Publication Data
Winter, Jane Kohen, 1959-
  Chile /Jane Kohen Winter and Susan Roraff. — 3rd ed.
      p. cm. — (Cultures of the world)
  Includes bibliographical references and index.
  Summary: "Provides comprehensive information on the geography, history,
  wildlife, governmental structure, economy, cultural diversity, peoples,
  religion, and culture of Chile"—Provided by publisher.
  ISBN 978-1-60870-800-0 (print) — ISBN 978-1-60870-807-9 (ebook)
1. Chile--Juvenile literature. I. Roraff, Susan. II. Title. III. Series.

F3058.5.W56 2012
983—dc23   2011025227

Printed in Malaysia
7 6 5 4 3 2 1

CONTENTS

CHILE TODAY

CHILE HAS A UNIQUE GEOGRAPHY AND OVERWHELMING NATURAL beauty. Nature is a fundamental part of any Chilean experience because such a great variety of it is crammed into this long, narrow country, which stretches down South America's western coast from the Peruvian border to the island of Tierra del Fuego. Chile also lays claim to a section of Antarctica, a continent where territorial issues remain unresolved. The result is a rich diversity of climates and landscapes: from subtropical to polar, from deserts to forests, and from mountains, volcanoes, and lakes to the elongated Pacific coastline. In the words of Nobel Prize-winning poet Gabriela Mistral, Chile has "naked rocks, hard jungle, vast orchards, snows, and icebergs last."

Northern Chile is dominated by the Atacama Desert, parts of which have not received a single drop of rain since people have been recording rainfall. Not only are there beautiful landscapes—salt flats, Moon Valley, an occasional oasis, high-altitude lakes, and volcanoes—but this area is also home to archaeological treasures such as mummies, geoglyphs (large drawings etched into mountainsides or onto the ground), and some of the oldest churches in the Americas. One of the country's

The dramatic Parinacota Volcano and Chungará Lake form part of the Lauca National Park in Chile.

most colorful festivals, the Festival of the Virgin of La Tirana, is celebrated in this northern town on July 16 every year.

Central Chile is known for its pleasant climate and fertile soil. Much of the produce grown here supplies the Northern Hemisphere with its fruits and vegetables during the northern winter season. Chile has perfect soil conditions for cultivating many different fruits, such as peaches, plums, grapes, and blueberries. Santiago is at the heart of this region, and even though it is a large city, nature is never far away. The snowcapped Andes Mountains tower over the city to the east, and the Coastal mountain range hugs the western part of the city. After a short drive out of the capital, whether to the north, south, or west, the traveler will come upon bucolic fields and lush vineyards. The coastal cities of Viña del Mar and Valparaíso can be reached in just a couple of hours.

The south possesses yet more spectacular scenery, particularly in the Lake District, where a visitor can gaze upon glaciers, volcanoes, lakes, waterfalls, and forests. Culturally, this region is interesting because the area around Temuco is home to so many of the country's indigenous Mapuche (mah-POO-chay) people. In addition, towns such as Valdivia, Puerto Varas, and Frutillar reveal a strong German presence in terms of food, architecture, and language.

The far south is notorious for its fierce winds, icy temperatures, and rough seas. Many travel to this region, called Patagonia—southern parts of Chile and Argentina—to see penguins or to visit one of the country's most beautiful parks, Torres del Paine. Set in the heart of southern Patagonia, the Torres del Paine National Park (declared a World UNESCO Biosphere Reserve in 1978) is one of the most impressive natural geographical spectacles on earth. The main city, Punta Arenas, is known for its brightly colored houses and significant Croatian influence.

Easter Island, a Polynesian island famous for its giant carved-stone figures of heads and torsos, called *moais* (moh-ays), and the Juan Fernández Archipelago, where the real Robinson Crusoe, Alexander Selkirk, lived as a castaway for some four years (1704—08), are also parts of Chilean territory.

Yet Chile is a very homogenous country. For the most part, Chileans share a common language, religion, and ethnic background. Throughout the country's history, various waves of immigrants from Spain, England, France, Italy, Germany, Croatia, and Palestine have assimilated well and become part of Chilean society, no different from their neighbors, distinguishable perhaps only by their family name. New surges of immigrants, for example from Korea and Peru, however, have had a harder time blending in and have retained more of their ethnic identity. This new immigration, combined with a growing expatriate community, has resulted in a perceptively more diverse society. Those walking down the street will now see people who look "different" and hear a number of different languages and regional Spanish accents. Used to having a somewhat closed society because of both geographical and political reasons, Chileans are now learning how to accept and live with others. While some growing pains may linger, overall these changes are peaceful.

Educated, artistic, and cosmopolitan, Chileans are also friendly and welcoming. As the country's economy has grown and become wealthier, there have been noticeable changes, especially in urban areas. There is a higher degree of sophistication, reflected in clothing, cultural activities, and culinary experimentation. Twenty years ago the vast majority of restaurants were Chilean. The only exotic restaurants were Chinese. Today there are Indian,

Glacial blue ice from the Grey Glacier in the gorgeous Torres del Paine National Park.

Countless Chilean beaches attract vacationing families.

Mexican, Ecuadorian, Russian, French, and Brazilian restaurants, and more. Chileans are increasingly venturing beyond their comfort zones and trying new things and visiting new places. It is a very exciting time to be in Chile, as the nation strives to become the first developed country in Latin America.

Their buildings and the infrastructure are a reflection of Chilean society. Santiago is now home to the tallest building in South America. There is a growing sense of confidence as Chile's presence in the global market is strengthened. New highways and bridges are being built on a continuous basis, constantly improving the ability to travel quickly and safely throughout the country.

In addition to attracting foreign investment and being a preferred location for international businesses, Chile has also made a name for itself as a great tourist destination. With its diverse geography, there really is something for everyone in Chile, be it a trip to a spa in the desert, a seaside sojourn, a cruise to the glaciers in the south, or camping in a national park. Luxury hotels and first-class experiences are to be found just as easily as cheaper options for backpackers on a budget. It remains one of the safest countries in Latin America, so it draws not only the adventure traveler but also retirees, families, single travelers, and study-abroad students.

The first thing a newcomer to Chile will discover, whether visitor or immigrant, is that Chileans are very proud of their country. It is common practice for Chileans to put themselves and their country down as backward, but they don't really mean it and expect you to protest in Chile's defense. In fact, they have many things to be proud of in addition to their beautiful country. Chileans elected the first woman president in South America, and Chile has returned to a stable democracy following the Pinochet dictatorship from 1973 to 1989. Poverty has dropped significantly since the return of democracy. Shantytowns have been almost completely eradicated, with most people living now in adequate housing with electricity, potable water, and sanitation.

Chile is fiscally responsible and weathered the 2008 financial crisis very well. Although Chile suffered an 8.8 earthquake in 2010, relative to other countries it experienced low loss of life. Perhaps one of the country's proudest moments was in October 2010 when 33 miners were rescued 70 days after a copper-gold mine collapsed in the north. The riveting rescue broadcast Chilean ingenuity and the ability of the government and private industry to work together for such an important common goal. Chile has produced two Nobel Prize winners for poetry and has made other significant contributions in the areas of art, music, and literature.

In spite of all the progress that has been made in Chile, however, there remain some areas that could be improved. Although the fight against poverty has shown some positive results, poverty remains an important issue in Chile, primarily in rural and indigenous communities. Relations with the indigenous Mapuche have suffered recently as seen in protests, some violent, against nonindigenous landowners and the police. Successive governments have been confronted with this social issue and are trying to determine the best way to address Mapuche demands. The quality of public education needs to be improved so that the poor have the same opportunities as the wealthy, who can afford to send their children to private schools. Environmental concerns are starting to have a higher priority on the national agenda, especially among younger citizens. Still, years of environmentally unfriendly practices will be hard to change overnight. Finally, rapid economic growth in Chile has brought with it some of the same problems faced by people in the United States and other developed countries. As people have become entangled in the rat race, they are experiencing higher stress levels, and the frantic impulse to keep up with the neighbors has seeped into the national consciousness.

All in all, Chileans are smart, resilient, and determined, and in time they will be able to overcome most of these problems. They have a great love for their country and will work hard to make it even better. Chileans tend not to emigrate in large numbers. Instead, they are devoted to their homeland and will invest in making it the best possible place to live. This is one of the main reasons why so many foreigners have chosen Chile as a place to visit, study, work, and live.

GEOGRAPHY

Lake Pehoe at Torres del Paine is a scenic spot of lush natural

CHILE IS THE LONGEST COUNTRY in the world. Though it stretches 2,700 miles (4,344 km) along the southwestern coast of the South American continent, its average width is only 110 miles (177 km). The 600-mile (965-km) long Atacama Desert stretches across northern Chile.

The Andes Mountains, covering a third of Chilean land, separate Chile from Argentina and Bolivia in the east. With an area of 292,136 square miles (756,630 square km), excluding the large Chilean claim over

The fertile landscape of Puerto Murta in the Aysen region of Patagonia.

Where Chile got its name remains a mystery, although there are at least six different explanations. Some of these stories trace the origin to an Amerindian language. Chile may have derived its name from a Peruvian Indian word that means "snow" or from an Inca word that means "where the land ends" or "the deepest point of the earth." Others believe that the name derives from the call of a bird, "*cheele-cheele.*"

After a rain, desert shrubs push through crevices in the hardened mud slabs of the Atacama Desert.

Antarctic territory, mainland Chile is slightly larger than the state of Texas. The Juan Fernández Archipelago and Easter Island in the South Pacific Ocean are also parts of Chile.

Chile is subject to extremes in weather due to winds, storms, and ocean currents. The country lies in a geologically active zone and is prone to earthquakes, floods, and volcanic eruptions. More than 100 earthquakes have been recorded since 1575, and these are sometimes followed by tidal waves, or tsunamis. Flash floods caused by the rapid melting of snow in the Andes can damage villages, and fishermen are always on the alert for sudden storms and strong currents. Major cities such as Valparaíso and Concepción have been damaged repeatedly by natural disasters. On February 27, 2010, Chile was struck by an earthquake that measured 8.8 on the Richter scale, one of the strongest ever recorded in history. Dozens of villages were destroyed and more than 500 people perished. While some buildings in the cities were damaged, many remained intact because of the strict building codes that prevented even worse devastation. In fact, most deaths were caused by the resulting tsunami that swamped coastal areas.

More than 50 active volcanoes are scattered throughout the landscape of the Andes mountain range down the entire length of Chile. Recent eruptions have included the Chaitén Volcano in 2008 that led to the evacuation of some 4,000 people of Chaitén in the south. The Lascar Volcano in the north and the Llaima Volcano and Puyehue Volcano near the Lake District have also experienced recent eruptions.

Chilean terrain ranges from the dry Atacama Desert in the north to the green central valley to the forested Lake District in the south to icy fjords and glaciers at the southernmost tip of the country. Because of Chile's length, daylight hours vary greatly. On the longest day of the year, December 23, Arica in the north sees about 13 hours of daylight, whereas Puerto Williams in the far south has 17 hours of daylight.

NORTHERN, CENTRAL, AND SOUTHERN CHILE

Chile is divided into three major geographic regions that differ dramatically in terms of population, climate, topography, and natural resources.

Northern Chile ranges south from the Peruvian border to the city of La Serena; it includes the bleak, thinly populated Atacama Desert and the coastal cities of Arica, Iquique, and Antofagasta. Northern Chile contains great deposits of gold and copper, which make important contributions to the nation's economy.

Central Chile lies between La Serena and Concepción and is the heartland of the country. Some 85 percent of the population lives in the major cities of this area. The capital, Santiago (also known as Santiago de Chile) has a population of over 6.25 million. The nearby Valparaíso Region (commonly referred to as the 5th Region), which includes the twin cities of Valparaíso-Viña del Mar, the second-largest port and a coastal resort area, has a population of 600,000. The Bío-Bío Region, which includes the Concepción-Talcahuano metropolitan area and other cities such as Los Angeles and Chillán, has a population of almost 2 million. The green and highly cultivated central region strikingly resembles the Central Valley of California.

The *Territorio Antártico Chileno*, or Chilean Antarctic Territory is an area in Antarctica claimed by Chile. It ranges from 53°W to 90°W and from the South Pole to 60°S, partially overlapping Argentine and British Antarctic claims and is administered by the Cabo de Hornos municipality on the South American mainland.

The Polloquere natural thermal springs, located in northern Chile, next to the Surire Salt Plain in Lauca National Park, is a popular tourist destination.

ASTRONOMY IN CHILE

The skies near La Serena are some of the clearest and driest in the world. Astronomers, astrophysicists, and other scientists flock to this area from across the globe to conduct research, making it the most important region in the Southern Hemisphere for astronomical observation. The landscape is dotted with excellent observatories that

are in such high demand that there are long waiting lists and high fees for using the facilities. Cerro Tololo Inter-American Observatory (right) is run by an association that includes the University of Chile and a number of American universities. La Silla Observatory is operated by the European Southern Observatory. Las Campanas Observatory is administered by the Carnegie Institute in Washington, D.C. Efforts are currently underway by a worldwide consortium to build the world's largest telescope, the Giant Magellan Telescope, due for completion in 2018.

Southern Chile begins south of Concepción and extends all the way to Cape Horn, South America's southernmost point. South of the Bío-Bío River lies Chile's Lake District, which has been likened to the Pacific Northwest of the United States in climate and to Switzerland for its scenic grandeur. The area contains deep-blue lakes, stunning glaciers, and lush forests, making it a prime vacation spot. Many of Chile's German immigrants and most of the remaining indigenous people—the Mapuche—live in the Lake District.

Southern Chile contains a maze of hundreds of small islands, dramatic fjords, and glaciers. Punta Arenas, the southernmost city and a major port, lies on the Strait of Magellan, which was an important passageway from the Atlantic to the Pacific prior to the opening of the Panama Canal in 1914. Across the strait lies the island of Tierra del Fuego, which is shared with Argentina. It is said that as Magellan sailed through the strait that now bears his name,

he and his men saw a number of small fires burning across the landscape as the native people warmed themselves. This spectacle led him to call the island Tierra del Fuego, or Land of Fire. Southern Chile has violent climatic conditions, with fierce storms, freezing rains, and cutting winds. This is why it is populated by only a small percentage of Chile's people, even though the region occupies more than one-third of the country's land area.

ISLANDS OF ADVENTURE

Easter Island and the Juan Fernández Archipelago in the southeastern Pacific Ocean are Chile's islands of adventure. Both territories have very interesting histories.

Easter Island is one of the world's most isolated islands and has an ancient and mysterious history. Acquired by Chile in 1888, this tiny island now has fewer than 4,000 inhabitants. While some are migrants from the mainland, the majority are Polynesian adventurers. This haven is also called Rapa Nui (Large Island) or Te Pito O Te Henua (Navel of the World). The island is chiefly known for its more than 887 ancient giant carved stone humanlike figures called *moais* that date as far back as A.D. 900. The figures have

Mystery surrounds these stone statues called *moais*. There are 600 of them on Easter Island. This stand of seven *moais* of Ahu Akivi represent, according to legend, the seven explorers sent by King Matu'a from Hiva, in the Marquesas Islands.

CHILOÉ ISLAND

Some 621 miles (1,000 km) south of the capital, Santiago, lies a very large island, Chiloé. This island, which still is accessible only by boat from the mainland, is unlike any other part of Chile. Homes and churches are painted in bright colors to beat back the cloudy skies and dreary rainfall. Many homes, called palafitos *(pal-ah-FEE-tohs), are built on stilts to accommodate high tides.*

elongated heads, protruding eyebrows and chins, and small mouths. Many have distended earlobes and carved ear ornaments. Some of the figures are only 7 feet (2 meters) high, whereas the tallest stands at a height of about 70 feet (21 m). As they are made of stone, even the smaller statues weigh many tons. The largest statue weighs from 145 to 165 tons (132 to 150 metric tons).

How these heavy figures were carved and transported to sites all around the island and why they were shaped as they were make up a lingering mystery. Traditionally, it has been suggested that the statues are representations of sacred chiefs or important figures. Experts agree that the *moais* were originally used as religious idols and later used to decorate and protect burial sites.

The major island in the Juan Fernández Archipelago is known as Robinson Crusoe Island. The real-life Crusoe, a Scottish sailor named Alexander Selkirk, was stranded on this island in 1704. The prolific English writer Daniel Defoe (1660—1731) modeled his hero after Selkirk but set his novel *Robinson Crusoe* (1719) thousands of miles away in the Caribbean Sea!

After an argument with his captain, Selkirk defiantly demanded to be cast ashore on the uninhabited island in the Juan Fernández group. As he disliked seafood, native goats became his major source of nourishment. When rescued four years later, he could barely still speak English and wore goatskin clothing. He became quite a celebrity when he reached London, but he said, "I shall never be so happy as when I was not worth a farthing." He even tried to build a cave behind his father's house in Scotland just like the one he had lived in on the island. He set off again for sea in 1717 and died from a fever on board a ship in 1723.

CLIMATE

Chile is located in the Southern Hemisphere, so the warmest months are December to March. In contrast, June, July, and August are the coldest and in most parts of the country, the wettest. Because of its length, Chile stretches across many climatic regions.

The Atacama Desert in the north is one of the driest places on earth; in many spots there, it rains only once a decade. Average high temperatures in the desert reach 72°F (22°C) in the winter and 86°F (30°C) in the summer, although they have been known to soar higher. The temperature drops at night, however, and in winter can fall below freezing.

Santiago, in the Central Valley, has a stable, Mediterranean climate. Average daytime high temperatures in the summer can reach 90°F (32°C) but

Llareta (yah-REH-tah), a dense, woody, moss-like plant, is part of the scanty vegetation that grows in the Atacama Desert of the northern Andes. *Llareta* is gathered for fuel.

can drop significantly at night. In the winter months, the average daytime high temperature is 57°F (14°C) and overnight temperatures seldom fall lower than 32°F (0°C). Therefore, it rarely snows in Santiago in the winter, and when it does, it snows only up in the higher elevations. Winter is the rainy season, and the average annual rainfall in the capital is 10.3 inches (26.2 cm). Precipitation is higher, 14.5 inches (37 cm), along the coast.

As one moves south, temperatures drop and rainfall increases. In the Lake District, the average daytime high temperature is 62°F (12.8°C) in the summer and 45°F (7°C) in winter. The average annual rainfall can be as high as 79 inches (200 cm). Strong winds blow year-round. In the southernmost town of Punta Arenas, the average annual temperature is 43°F (6.1°C). Some places in Patagonia have an average rainfall of 157.5 inches (400 cm) a year, but even higher amounts have been recorded. There is little seasonal change in these regions. In some areas bad weather is so unrelenting that such place names as Hill of Anguish and Ice Water Valley are commonly found.

FLORA AND FAUNA

The Atacama Desert has almost no plant life because of the lack of rain. At high altitudes certain species of cactus manage to survive by absorbing water from the fog, called *camanchaca* (kah-mahn-CHA-kah), which rolls in from the Pacific Ocean and blankets the peaks. The candleholder cactus, which is found at 6,000 feet (1,829 m), grows less than an inch (2.5 cm) a year.

Animal life in the Atacama Desert is just as scarce, but a seagull called the gray gull is known to nest in the desert. When one parent gull flies to the seacoast to hunt for food, the mate stands sentinel over their chick to shield it from the scorching sun. Gray gulls are said to pant like dogs during

THE ANDES AND MOUNTAIN SICKNESS

The lone geographic feature that unifies the diverse regions of Chile is the Andes mountain range. Some of Chile's peaks are taller than the highest mountains in Europe, Africa, and the United States. The Ojos del Salado, for instance, is 22,590 feet (6,885 m) tall, 2,270 feet (692 m) taller than Mount McKinley in Alaska (20,320 feet/6,194 m), the tallest mountain in the United States.

Mountain sickness, or soroche (soh-ROH-cheh), can occur at altitudes of 10,000 feet (3,048 m) and is totally random in its choice of victims. Hikers who have never had altitude sickness before can suddenly come down with it. Mountain sickness is rarely fatal but is usually extremely uncomfortable. Stricken climbers complain of headaches, a sudden lack of coordination, shortness of breath, stomach upset, and a kind of drunken feeling. This occurs because the air at high altitudes contains less oxygen.

There are individuals, nevertheless, who can live at high altitudes. They have adapted physiologically to their rarified environment. Thus, they have larger lungs and more blood in their system than people living at lower altitudes. Their hearts are also reportedly 20 percent larger!

The surest cure for severe mountain sickness is to descend to a lower altitude. In mild cases, the victim should rest for three or four days to allow the circulatory system to adjust. In Peru, Bolivia, and Ecuador, the customary cure for soroche is herbal tea made from coca leaves.

the hottest part of the day. Pink flamingos are also found in the Atacama Salt Flats in the midst of the desert, where they feed on krill, minute animal life.

Alpacas, vicuñas, and llamas prosper at higher altitudes. They are members of the camel family and have lived in South America for 2 to 3 million years. With the exception of the vicuña, these animals have been domesticated and cannot live apart from humans, who tend them for their milk, meat, and fleece. The very soft wool from these animals is woven into handsome garments.

The rich soil of the Central Valley is perfect for cultivating grains, vegetables, and fruits, such as grapes. Common trees here include the Chilean palm, poplar, weeping willow, and eucalyptus. South of Concepción, almost half the land is covered by forest. Chile's national flower, the copihue (koh-PEE-hway) of the lily family, grows in the wild in the Temuco area from October to July. The araucaria (ah-rhau-CAR-ee-ah) or monkey puzzle tree, an evergreen, grows south of the Bío-Bío River. Its high-quality wood is free of knots, making it an ideal substance for carving.

Birds such as the black-necked swan, wild goose, penguin, and condor, whose imposing wingspan can reach 10 feet (3 m), populate the southern regions of Patagonia and Magallanes. Pumas, red foxes, and small llamas called guanacos are plentiful in these regions.

The Chilean pudu, or dwarf deer, lives in the rain forests and lower Andes Mountains of southern Chile. Measuring only 15 inches (38 cm) tall

Monkey puzzle and southern beech trees at the lava-dammed lake in Conguillo National Park in the Araucania region.

and weighing less than 25 pounds (11.3 kg) when fully grown, the pudu is the world's smallest deer. Pudus resemble tiny antelopes with fox-like faces and spotted coats. They are solitary and travel alone. Their diet consists of leaves and berries. At one time pudus were common in parts of the Chilean and Argentine Andes. Now their numbers are regrettably scarce, and they have become an endangered species in the region.

An abundant array of fish and seafood from the Pacific Ocean is found along Chile's western coast. Some of the most important species include tuna, swordfish, sole, smelt, sardine, mackerel, red and black conger eel (which are a national culinary specialty), in addition to octopus, shrimp, clam, crab, mussel, sea urchin, and abalone. Lobster can be found near the Juan Fernández Archipelago. Salmon and trout live in rivers and lakes.

"The sense of sublimity, which the…forest-clad mountains of Tierra del Fuego excited in me…has left an indelible impression on my mind."—Charles Darwin, in *Voyage of the Beagle*

INTERNET LINKS

http://travel.nationalgeographic.com/travel/countries/chile-guide/?source=A-to-Z

This popular magazine's website provides facts, guides, maps, and photos of Chile. This enchanting site has some of the most beautiful and most interesting photographs of Chile.

www.thisischile.cl/Articles.aspx?id=1201&sec=356&eje=x&itz=&t=geography-chile&idioma=2

This is the official government website with information on all aspects of Chile. The section entitled Nature and Geography discusses Chile's climate, geography, natural parks, nature reserves, and flora and fauna.

www.geographia.com/chile/

This website provides information on Chile's varied geography. It covers the role of geography in the history of the country and provides detailed information on a large number of Chile's main cities.

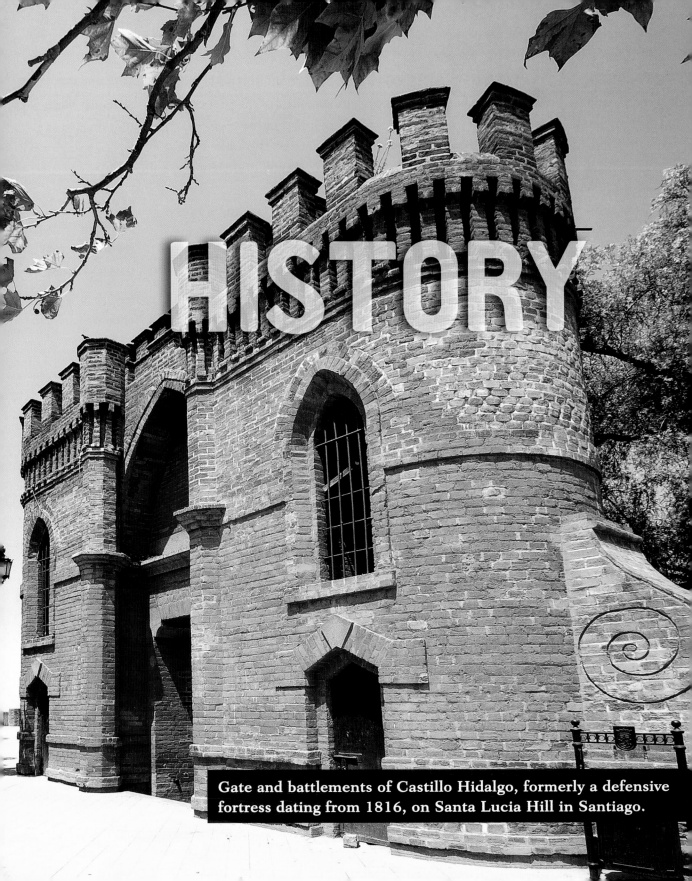

HISTORY

Gate and battlements of Castillo Hidalgo, formerly a defensive
fortress dating from 1816, on Santa Lucia Hill in Santiago.

ARCHAEOLOGICAL DISCOVERIES at Monte Verde suggest that parts of Chile were inhabited as early as 14,500 years ago, although this claim is sometimes disputed. Some 3,500 years later, the Atacameños arrived in the area north of the Atacama Salt Flat. They lived as hunter-gatherers until about 1500 B.C., when they began to farm and set up permanent villages.

Archaeologists have also studied the Chinchorro culture, which existed in Chile between 7000 and 500 B.C. Many mummies and tools of the Chinchorro have been unearthed in sites near Arica.Some of them are more than 7,000 years old. Studies done on these mummies reveal that many of the Chinchorro men probably went deaf from diving for shellfish, whereas the women had an unusual arthritis of the neck from carrying heavy loads. Tools found at the sites, such as nets and harpoons, indicate that the Chinchorro were skilled fishermen.

In 1954 gold miners in the Chilean Andes near Santiago stumbled across the perfectly preserved 500-year-old body of an Incan boy around 9 years of age. Scientists believe the boy was of noble birth and was sacrificed to the Sun God during a festival. His mummy is on display at the National Museum of Natural History in Santiago.

Right: A mummy displayed in the Museo Regional de Atacama in Copiapó.

> "(T)his land is such that there is none better in the world."
> —Pedro de Valdivia, Spanish conquistador, writing about Chile in a letter to his king.

The Atacameño group left numerous geoglyphs strewn across the Atacama Desert over an area of more than 100 square miles (259 square km). These geoglyphs depict animals such as llamas, lizards, cats, birds, and fish. The smallest drawing is about 3.3-feet (1-m) tall, and the largest, the Atacama Giant, is about 380 feet (116 m) in height. These mysterious images were drawn along an old Andean trade route. Thousand-year-old mummies of the Atacameño culture have also been found.

The Diaguitas also lived in the north, although their numbers dropped drastically following the arrival of the Spanish. Their culture lives on in their pottery, often described as the best of all the Chilean indigenous groups' work.

A number of indigenous peoples lived in the extreme south, including the Chonos, Kawesqar, Aonikenk, Selk'nam, and Yagan. Because of the cold temperatures, many indigenous tribes wore thick animal pelts on their feet. The Spaniards called them Patagones, or "big feet," giving the region the name of Patagonia.

SPANISH CONQUEST

In the 1400s Incas from Peru ventured across Chile's northern desert and took control of the northern half of what is now the Central Valley. Their attempts to claim more territory in the south were foiled by the Mapuche, also known as Araucanians, who resisted the invaders with great ferocity. In the mid-16th century, at the time of the Spanish conquest, the country had some 1 million Indians from several different groups.

The Portuguese explorer Fernando de Magallanes—or Ferdinand Magellan, as he is called in English—sailed through what is now called the Strait of Magellan in 1520. He was the first European to see the southern region called Tierra del Fuego. In about 1535 Spanish conquistador Diego de Almagro came down to Chile from Peru in search of gold and silver. He got as far as what is now Santiago before turning back. The town of Santiago was officially founded by Spaniard Pedro de Valdivia in 1541.

The Mapuche were one of the few indigenous New World groups to win repeated battles against the Spanish. Valdivia himself was killed by the Mapuche in 1553. They were clever warriors who stole Spanish horses, using them to raid Spanish towns. Eventually, the Mapuche men gave up farm life and devoted themselves to warfare.

An artist's impression of the early Indian community in Patagonia.

Despite their success in war, the Mapuche were not as materially sophisticated as the Incas. They did not build cities and had few advanced tools. They lived in simple one-room huts called *rucas* (ROO-kahs) made from wooden poles, straw, and animal skins. Their language was complex, however, as well as their spiritual world. They loved sports, especially a game called *chueca* (CHWAY-kah), which resembles field hockey. In the mid-17th century, the Indians signed a peace treaty with the Spanish, but the hawkish Mapuche were not really quelled until the late 1800s.

Before he died, Valdivia divided much of the agricultural land in Chile among his soldiers and gave them Indian slaves to farm the land in a traditional Spanish system called the *encomienda* (ehn-KOH-mee-EHN-dah). When slavery was outlawed, Indians became tenant farmers, or *inquilinos* (een-kee-LEE-nos), on large plantations, or haciendas.

Each hacienda or *fundo* (FOON-doh) was a society unto itself. It had its own store, church, and sometimes a school. Indians lived in huts on the estate, kept some livestock, and had small patches of land to grow food for their families.

During the colonial period Chile was run by a governor who answered to the viceroyalty of Peru in Lima. The Spanish authority forbade Chile to trade with the other Spanish colonies, and this led to smuggling. Because of various such restraints imposed on the Chileans, many landowners gradually abandoned their fidelity to Spain, which had little interest in a remote land with scarce gold resources and an indomitable group of indigenous people.

Pedro de Valdivia, the Spanish explorer who founded the city of Santiago, now the capital of Chile.

THE INDEPENDENCE MOVEMENT

In the early 19th century Spain controlled territory stretching from California in the north to Cape Horn in the south, from the Pacific Ocean in the west to the mouth of Venezuela's Orinoco River in the east. Less than 20 years later, the only Spanish colonies left were Cuba and Puerto Rico.

The disappearance of Spanish colonies was the outcome of independence movements igniting all over Latin America. These populist movements came about for several reasons. The Spanish held their colonies back from economic prosperity by imposing strict trade laws. Many Spaniards born in the New World considered themselves to be more South American than Spanish. They drew zeal and inspiration from the American and French independence movements of the late 1700s.

On September 18, 1810, the first autonomous Chilean government was declared within the Spanish monarchy, but Spain later reclaimed Chile. Not until Argentine-born José de San Martín and his army made their way into Chile from Argentina in 1817 that the final victory came into view. Claiming that he "came to liberate Chile, not to rule it," San Martín appointed a Chilean general of his army, Bernardo O'Higgins, the son of an influential Irish immigrant and a Chilean woman of the Spanish colonists, as head of the new government. Independence was officially proclaimed on February 12,

1818, but Independence Day is celebrated on September 18 every year.

Bernardo O'Higgins, the father of Chile's independence, was an intellectual interested in making cultural, economic, and educational progress in Chile, notably among the poor. He built schools, a library, and lighting and sanitation systems in Santiago. Wealthy landowners, who continued to influence Chilean politics and society, and the leaders of the Roman Catholic Church did not approve of O'Higgins. He was ousted in 1823 and went into exile in Peru, where he died in 1842 without ever seeing his beloved Chile again.

In the civil war that raged between 1829 to 1830, the conservative landowners won. That war was between them and the liberals, headed by President Ramón Freire, who ruled from 1826 to 1830. In 1833 Chile adopted a constitution that highly centralized the government, granting the president direct control over the provinces.

The father of Chile's independence, Bernardo O'Higgins.

THE 19TH CENTURY

By the 19th century Chile had won the War of the Pacific (1879—83) against Peru and Bolivia. The victory expanded the country's territory by a third and gave it possession of the Atacama Desert, which had rich deposits of nitrate, a natural fertilizer. The exportation of nitrate gave Chile an important source of income for 40 years, and the mining industry created stable jobs for a new group that soon became the middle class. Bolivia lost its access to the Pacific Ocean following its defeat, and this shut-out continues to be a hot potato in Chilean-Bolivian diplomatic relations to this day.

President José Manuel Balmaceda, who took office in 1886, was the first leader to attempt to place some of the country's wealth in the hands of the middle class. The Chilean upper class and the British, Chile's important trading partner, disliked Balmaceda's policies for social reform, and another civil war erupted. It was a very bloody period in Chile's history—10,000 Chileans lost their lives. Balmaceda was ousted in 1891.

MODERN CHILE

A socialist, as president (1970-1973) Salvador Allende Gossens was a passionate reformer.

In 1920 Arturo Alessandri was elected by the working and middle classes in another attempt to reduce the power of landowners and shrink the gap between rich and poor. Alessandri was ousted by a military takeover in 1924 but returned to power in 1925. He wrote a new constitution that separated church from state, authorized tax reforms, and ensured freedom of worship, and declared new laws to empower the poor. Literate males over 21 were given the right to vote (women's suffrage did not come about until 1940). The 1925 Alessandri constitution governed politics in Chile until 1973.

The 1930s were marked by the worldwide Great Depression and a fall in nitrate prices after the invention of artificial nitrates. Many political parties were created in this period. Despite the turmoil, Chile was considered the most steadfast democracy in South America. Elections were held regularly, and the press had great freedom.

In 1964 Eduardo Frei Montalva was elected to the presidency, the first Christian Democratic candidate to ever win a presidential election in Latin America. Frei began far-reaching social programs for the poor in housing, education, and land redistribution. During his time in office, unfortunately, unemployment and inflation rose.

Salvador Allende, a Marxist and member of the Socialist Party, was elected president in 1970 by a narrow margin. His aim and that of his Popular Unity coalition was to transform Chile into a socialist state. He took over many of Chile's privately owned industries and banks and redistributed land owned by the upper class. During his last year in power the economy faltered and inflation soared. A harsh ideological confrontation ensued. There were mass demonstrations, strikes, and widespread unrest fueled by shortages of food and consumer goods.

In a violent coup d'état on September 11, 1973, the military—consisting of the army, air force, navy, and national police—overthrew the Allende

PINOCHET AND HUMAN RIGHTS

The Pinochet regime has been accused of many human rights abuses. Augusto Pinochet's government went far beyond curbing basic democratic freedoms, such as the rights to congregate and to have an independent press, to actively and violently striking out to rid the country of communists and any other type of dissention. In the early years of the military government, DINA, Chile's secret police at that time, was responsible for widespread repression within the country. It was even behind the assassinations of high-profile Chilean nationals in foreign countries, for example Orlando Letelier (and his U.S. colleague Ronni Moffitt) in the United States and General Carlos Prat and his wife in Argentina. Many citizens suspected of opposing the government were jailed, sent to prison camps, tortured, and/or murdered. Many Chileans simply disappeared, and their families never heard from them again. These have come to be known as "the disappeared" and estimates of their numbers range from 2,000 to 6,000 individuals. Many more Chileans were forcibly exiled or fled the country for their lives. Sizable Chilean communities settled in countries such as Sweden, East Germany, Mexico, and Canada, among others.

When Pinochet gave up power, he tried to ensure that none of his soldiers or police would be tried for human rights abuses by enacting an amnesty law. President Patricio Alwyin set up the Chilean National Commission on Truth and Reconciliation to investigate the abuses. When Pinochet was visiting England in 1998, a Spanish judge ordered his arrest and requested his extradition for human rights crimes. The British government placed him under house arrest while the courts ruled on the matter. After more than a year, it was decided that he was too ill to stand trial and he was allowed to return to Chile. Pinochet supporters, who still made up almost 40 percent of the population, came out to welcome him home, while many, including the families of the disappeared, protested and called for his arrest in Chile.

Despite the warm welcome by his supporters, Pinochet had returned to a different Chile. In June 2000 he was stripped of immunity against prosecution granted by his position as senator-for-life and was named in over 250 human rights cases. In July 2001, 85-year-old Pinochet was saved by his failing health when the appeals court in Santiago ruled that he was unfit to stand trial. Pinochet died in 2006, a hero to some Chileans and a cruel despot to many others.

government. It was later revealed that the U.S. government, through the Central Intelligence Agency (CIA), had played a part in destabilizing the Allende government and in the subsequent military overthrow. The presidential palace was attacked, and the president and his supporters stood their ground. During the coup, however, Allende died, having committed suicide. Although Salvador Allende's term was short, he left a permanent legacy in Chile for his attempts at social reform and for what many consider his martyrdom.

Immediately following the coup, Chile was ruled by a junta, or a small group of leaders, made up of the commanders in chief of the four military forces. Eventually, General Augusto Pinochet, head of the army, emerged as the dominant executive. He chose his cabinet, and his government appointed regional administrators, provincial governors, mayors, and rectors of state universities. Congress was shut down, and the general outlawed political parties and labor unions and instituted a curfew. The press was tightly controlled. The economy had suffered greatly under Allende, so Pinochet focused on restoring economic stability to the country. His government

Armed guards watch for attackers as President Salvador Allende leaves the Moneda presidential palace during the military coup in which he was overthrown and later died.

implemented strict economic policies that promoted a free market economy with limited state involvement. These policies were successful in bringing down inflation, but relief came with a price. There was high foreign debt, high unemployment rates, and high levels of poverty. Workers protested, but they were subject to harsh government reprisals. Many analysts argue that such types of severe economic policies are not possible in democracies.

General Augusto Pinochet (*first from left*), along with his junta leaders, a year after the Allende fall.

INTERNET LINKS

www.history.com/topics/chile

This website, related to the History Channel, offers many facts on Chile's development as a country. It incorporates how various issues have affected the country's history, including geography, climate, and soil quality. It also provides information on the people who have played central roles in the country's history.

http://countrystudies.us/chile/

This site has many entries on specific periods in Chilean history, ranging from pre-Columbian civilizations through the colonial period, and Chile's entire history as an independent nation.

www.derechoschile.com/english/about.htm

Derechos Chile is a website that provides a great deal of detailed information on human rights issues, both past and present, in Chile.

www.theancientweb.com/explore/content.aspx?content_id=7

This website provides information on the ancient cultures of Patagonia, the Incas, and the Ona, or Selk'nam, people of southern Chile. It also offers detailed accounts of Mapuche history.

In 1979 Chile was on the brink of war with Argentina due to border disputes in the far south. Conflict was averted, and the issue was resolved with the intervention of Pope John Paul II at the request of both countries.

GOVERNMENT

Supporters of the Chilean right-wing opposition alliance's presidential candidate Sebastián Piñera celebrate in the streets of Santiago after hearing the news of his win.

CHILEAN GOVERNMENTS HAVE always been highly centralized with a strong presidency. In other words, power is primarily held by the central government, located in Santiago and Valparaíso, and many decisions are made by the president. Until 1973 Chile had been considered one of the most stable democracies in South America.

When the democratically elected government of Salvador Allende was overthrown by the armed forces in September of that year, most believed the military would hand power back to the politicians within a short period of time. Many initial supporters of the coup d'état did not expect General Augusto Pinochet to cling to power for 17 long years.

In 1988, anticipating a victory that would consolidate his legacy, Pinochet allowed Chileans to decide whether he should remain their chief executive for another eight years. He was defeated when 55 percent voted in favor of a presidential election, which was then held in 1989. The pro-Pinochet candidate, Hernan Büchi, lost, and the general had to transfer the presidential office to a democratic politician, Patricio Aylwin. Thousands of cheering Chileans thronged the streets of Santiago to celebrate the demise of the dictatorship.

RETURN TO DEMOCRACY

Patricio Aylwin, the leader of the Christian Democratic Party, was considered a moderate, the person who could lead Chile best in its

Michelle Bachelet, the outgoing president of Chile, (*front left*) and Sebastián Piñera (*far right*), the new president, stand during the 2010 inauguration ceremony at the National Congress in Valparaíso.

transition to democracy. When he took office, leading the Concertación (kohn-sehr-tah-see-OHN), a union of center and left-wing democratic political parties, he stated that his priorities would be to convict those responsible for human rights crimes, maintain economic stability, and narrow the gap between rich and poor. He immediately reinstated full press and political freedoms, supported the release of political prisoners, and abolished the practice of exile. At the same time, Aylwin's government chose to continue many of the economic programs implemented by the Pinochet government.

Elections were held again in 1993, and Christian Democrat Eduardo Frei Ruiz-Tagle, the Concertación candidate and son of President Eduardo Frei Montalva, won and took office in 1994. Then in 1999 Ricardo Lagos, also representing the Concertación, became the first socialist to be elected president since Allende. His government continued the policies of the two previous governments. When he left office in 2006, he had approval ratings of over 70 percent, an astonishingly high number. Under Chilean law a president cannot run for immediate reelection, so he could not continue as president in spite of his popularity. President Lagos was the last president to serve a six-year term, because a constitutional amendment has reset the presidential term at four years.

Dr. Michelle Bachelet, a pediatrician and a member of the Socialist Party, in 2005 became the first woman to be elected president of Chile. The daughter of an air force general who was arrested by the Pinochet regime and died while being held prisoner. She herself was arrested and sent into exile. She lived in Australia and East Germany before returning to Chile in 1979. She served as minister of health and later as minister of defense in the Lagos government. She was well liked and respected by the military. Her election was also notable in that she was separated from her husband, a single mother, and a declared agnostic in a very Roman Catholic country. After some problems surrounding the introduction of a new public transit system, she regained her popularity and left office with an 84 percent approval rating, the highest ever of any Chilean president. In September 2010 she was appointed Under Secretary General of the United Nations Entity for Gender Equality and the Empowerment of Women (UN Women) organization.

During the 2009 presidential elections it became clear that many Chileans were ready for a change after 20 years of rule by the center-left Concertación coalition. Sebastián Piñera, from the right-wing Renovación Nacional (National Renewal) party, ran against former President Eduardo Frei Ruiz-Tagle and won. Many saw his election and the peaceful transfer of power to the right as a sign of a mature democracy. Piñera is a very wealthy businessman with vested interests in many aspects of the Chilean economy (most of which were placed in a blind trust for the duration of his presidency). Many of his cabinet ministers are also immensely successful business leaders. He took power only days after a massive 8.8 earthquake, and his first year was mostly committed to rebuilding the country.

La Moneda, the presidential palace in Santiago, was originally built as a mint, thus the source of its name, which means "coinage."

THE LEGISLATURE

The Republic of Chile is headed by a chief executive, the president, who is elected for a four-year, nonrenewable term, although he or she may be reelected later. The president is head of both the state and government. In Santiago a stately palace, La Moneda, is the seat of the president. It also houses the offices of three cabinet ministers. The president appoints his or her cabinet ministers.

The seat of the legislative branch of the government was moved to the city of Valparaíso by the Pinochet government. The legislature is made up of two houses, the Senate and the Chamber of Deputies. Senators are elected for eight-year terms and deputies for four-year terms. There are 38 senators and 120 deputies. Half of the Senate is up for reelection every four years.

Chile's political party system is dominated on the center-right by UDI (Democratic Independent Union) and RN (National Renovation Party). The center-left is represented by the Socialist Party, the PPD (Party for Democracy), and the Christian Democratic Party (PDC). The Communist Party (PC) is the main group on the traditional left. There are some very small regional and independent political associations. Even though political parties were banned under the Pinochet government, opposition groups remained active underground and reappeared center stage with the return to democracy. Political party loyalty is strong in Chile, although formal membership is low.

THE JUDICIARY

Once a citizen registers to vote in Chile, he or she is legally obligated to vote in every election thereafter. As a result, some people choose not to register at all. Those who have registered but do not vote face fines. There are calls to make voter registration automatic at age 18, and then voting would be voluntary.

Chile's legal system is civil law that is based on codes instead of on rulings and precedents. The Supreme Court is the high court of the judicial branch of the government. Supreme Court judges are appointed for life by the president. Chile's 11 courts of appeal consist of judges appointed by the president from a list made up by Supreme Court judges. Similarly, judges of lower courts are chosen by the president from a list compiled by judges of the courts of appeal. Beginning in 2000 Chile underwent a total transformation of its criminal justice system. Criminal trials used to be written, secret, and inquisitional, but now are oral and adversarial. Rulings are made by judges. There are no juries. There is an independent system of public prosecutors (Ministerio Público) and a system of public defenders.

REGIONAL ADMINISTRATION

There are 15 regions in Chile administered by *intendentes*, or intendants, appointed by the president. There is also an appointed regional council. These regions are divided into provinces administered by governors. The provinces are further divided into municipalities managed by mayors, who are directly elected by the people. Municipal council members are also directly elected by the public.

FOREIGN POLICY

Following the return to democracy, Chile, being a relatively small country, has played an active role on the world stage. A firm believer in international law, it has been a founding member of several multilateral organizations and treaties and has made human rights a high priority in its foreign policy. A strong supporter of the United Nations, Chile's most important recent contribution has been its strong presence in the UN-led mission in Haiti in terms of the reconstruction efforts after the 2010 earthquake.

The courts of justice in Santiago.

INTERNET LINKS

https://www.cia.gov/library/publications/the-world-factbook/geos/ci.html

The CIA publishes the World Factbook with detailed information on each country's government, economy, military, people, and other interests. The entry on Chile provides valuable up-to-date information.

www.gobiernodechile.cl/english/

This is the official site of the Chilean government. There are many articles that report current events in Chile, the government's political positions on far-ranging issues, and official programs and policies.

http://chile.usembassy.gov/

This is the official website of the U.S. government regarding its relations with Chile. The site provides information on currents in political relations between the two countries.

ECONOMY

Cutting-edge architecture is seen in the Torre Titanium La Portada and Isidora Goyenechea skyscapers in Vitacura, the financial district of Santiago.

4

CHILE HAS ONE OF THE healthiest economies in Latin America. Inflation is low, and the country has the highest savings rate in the region. It is part of the global economy, nevertheless, and does feel the effects of international economic events. Chile was hit by the Asian economic crisis in 1998.

Due to restrained spending, however, and the introduction of restrictions on speculative capital flows in the years following 1998, Chile was not strongly affected by the 2008 global financial crisis. It was able to dip into its reserves to avoid a slowdown.

Much of Chile's success can be attributed to extensive exportation of local goods. Chile exports more than 5,000 products to over 190 countries. Chile sustained high growth rates until the 2008 financial crisis struck. As other countries reduced consumption, the value of Chile's 2009 exports dropped by 27 percent. A portion of that decline was due to lower demand for Chilean goods, while lower prices for commodities, especially the country's main export, copper, also contributed to the drop.

Fruit and vegetables are exported to the Northern Hemisphere, taking advantage of the fact that Chile's summer growing season is the winter season in the north. Other exports include salmon, wine, pork, fish meal, and cellulose products. In addition to manufactured goods, the country has also started to export services to other Latin American countries.

During the military dictatorship poverty rose dramatically, and some one-third of all Chileans were living below the poverty line. The

The Chilean economy is recurrently ranked among the best managed in the world, and the government is making a determined effort to raise the country's standing to that of a developed nation.

Cargo containers held at Valparaíso, the principal port of the country.

subsequent democratic governments continued with Pinochet's economic policies, but implemented significant social programs. Today, the rate of poverty has dropped to about 11.5 percent. Practically every Chilean has access to clean drinking water and electricity. Although government housing programs have eradicated most shantytowns, about 3.7 percent of the population is considered indigent, or extremely poor. Many people have had to create their own jobs to survive. Chileans who are not formally employed peddle cheap goods in the streets, clean car windshields, scour the city for discarded newspapers to sell to recycling centers, or stand guard at parked cars for cash. This economic behavior is known as the informal market.

Although Chile has a significant poor population, their condition is better than in many other developing countries. Most Chileans have enjoyed a rise in their standard of living, and there is now a sizable middle class. They have television sets, cars, and own their homes. Many have joined private pension and health-care plans, which is not common in Latin America.

EXPORTS AND FOREIGN INVESTMENTS

In 2010 the per capita income in Chile was estimated to be approximately $15,400. The gross domestic product (GDP) in the same year totaled $258 billion. The agricultural sector made up some 5.6 percent of the GDP. The services sector accounted for almost 53.9 percent of the GDP, whereas the industrial and manufacturing sectors brought in 40.5 percent. The main industrial activities were concentrated in textiles, metal manufacturing, food processing, and pulp, paper, and other wood products.

ENERGY

Energy is needed for development. Regrettably, Chile has limited energy resources. Coal used to be mined near Lota, but those mines have been closed. Chile has had to import the vast majority of natural gas and crude oil that it uses. In an effort to free itself from dependence on foreign energy, Chile has turned to hydroelectric production (dams), which has met strong environmental opposition, both national and international. Energy companies are looking ahead to new sources of energy to tackle the problem, such as wind farms, solar energy, and biofuels. The largest wind farm in South America is being planned for northern Chile.

Chile's exports in 2010 were worth some $64.28 billion. Major export products included copper, fruit, fish meal, and cellulose. The country's main trading partners are China, the United States, Japan, South Korea, the European Union, Peru, Mexico, Argentina, and Brazil. Major imports include industrial equipment, petroleum, chemical products, electronics, cars and trucks, and consumer goods.

Chile enjoys a high level of foreign investment. Most such investments are made in the mining sector, where Canada is the leading partner. Other affiliations are in communications, construction, forestry, and fishing. The United States is the biggest overall investor. Chile claims to have the most free trade agreements (57) with countries on all continents.

MINING

Mining is a significant source of revenue for Chile. Minerals make up about 60 percent of total exports. Copper is Chile's single most important source of wealth, accounting for one-third of all government revenues. Chile has about 20 percent of the world's copper reserves and has been the world's largest producer of copper since 1982. The most important copper mine, Chuquicamata, is the world's second-largest open-pit mine at over 2.48 miles (4 km) long, 1.86 miles (3 km) wide, and 2,953 feet (900 m) deep.

Chile also produces other metallic elements such as molybdenum, iron ore, and manganese, as well as sulfur, and nitrates. The Atacama Desert has the world's largest natural nitrate deposit, once a major source of revenue. Chile

The Chiquicamata open-pit copper mine in the Atacama Desert is the most important copper mine in Chile.

is the leading producer of lithium, making up over 40 percent of world reserves, and is a chief supplier of iodine.

Chile received awesome international respect and admiration with its thrilling rescue of 33 trapped miners in October 2010. The miners had been trapped underground for 70 days in the San José mine in Copiapó. Mining remains a dangerous profession, particularly in smaller mines.

MANUFACTURING AND INDUSTRY

Accounting for about 40 percent of GDP, the industrial and manufacturing sector remains an important component of the Chilean economy. Products from this sector include wine and beverages, wood products, food products, metal products, textiles, plastics, chemicals, and leather and shoes. These are mostly exported to the United States, other Latin American countries, and Japan. Manufacturing jobs are located primarily in the cities of Santiago, Valparaíso, and Concepción.

AGRICULTURE

Most of the farming in Chile takes place in the fertile 600-mile-long (966-km-long) Central Valley. Major agricultural products include potatoes, onions, garlic, sugar beets, wheat, fresh fruit (kiwi, apples, grapes, avocados, peaches, cherries, and blueberries), and fresh vegetables (asparagus, corn, and beans). The United States and Canada are major importers of Chilean produce. Because Chile is located south of the equator, it can put summer fruits such as grapes, peaches, and berries on North American tables in winter. Livestock production is limited to beef, poultry, and pork. Sheep are raised on farms in the southern regions of the country, where wool is another valuable commodity.

CARMENÈRE WINE

The Carmenère grape is Chile's signature variety. This grape became extinct in Europe in the 1860s when phylloxera, plant lice, struck the vineyards. It was believed to be gone forever. In 1994, however, it was discovered that Chilean grapes thought to be Merlot were actually Carmenère grapes. Chilean winemakers seized the opportunity and began to produce Carmenère wines. These high quality wines made from red grapes with the deepest purple hue have become very popular around the globe. Carmenère wines continue to win medals in international competitions.

FORESTRY AND FISHING

Chile is one of the world's top fishing nations. Traditional fishing accounts for the majority of production. Most fishing is done off the northern coast, where the main product is fish meal, used as animal feed. Fish and shellfish for human consumption are taken off the coast in central and southern Chile. Salmon, a major player in the economy, is raised on fish farms in the south. Chile is the world's second-largest producer of salmon.

Chile has more than a million acres (404,700 ha) of pine tree plantations, mostly located in the south, where the climate is more conducive to the growth of this evergreen. Most of the pine harvest is used to make pulp and paper products.

CHILE'S WINE INDUSTRY

The fertile lands located in the Central Valley are among the most exciting wine regions in the world. Many white wines are produced in the Casablanca Valley, just west of Santiago. Another important wine region is about a three-hour drive south of Santiago, near the town of Santa Cruz. Chile has an ideal climate, irrigation, and soil quality for growing grapes, and no harmful insects.

Unlike some other Latin American countries, Chile is not an accomplice in the international drug trade. To be sure, some communities are struggling with drug abuse, but Chile is not a major grower, producer, or exporter of illegal drugs.

The Morande flourishing vineyards in Chile, where wine production has skyrocketed in recent years.

Vines were originally planted by monks in Chile in the 1500s to make wine for the Eucharist in the Roman Catholic Mass. In the mid-1850s a Chilean wine grower employed a French wine specialist to grow grapes that would yield fine wines. By 1889 Chilean wines were winning important prizes in Paris.

Today, Chile is the largest exporter of wines in Latin America. It exports to more than 50 countries, including Japan, the United States, Canada, Great Britain, Colombia, Venezuela, Argentina, and Brazil. Chilean wines have an international reputation for having a good quality at a good value. Wine has steadily increased in importance in the Chilean economy, supplying both export revenue and jobs; wine exports grew dramatically from $13 million in 1986 to over $1.3 billion in 2009.

THE CHILEAN WORKDAY

The typical Chilean workday starts at 9 A.M., as in the United States, and ends at 6 P.M., although many people often work until 7 or 8 P.M. Yet Chileans do not take particularly long lunch hours. Metropolitan stores are usually open only half a day on Saturday. Nearly everything is closed on Sunday, except at the new megamalls, which stay open late, seven days a week.

Chilean businesspeople are generally conservative. They are known to be trustworthy and honorable when making deals. Women are taken seriously in the workforce and need not be overly aggressive to have their opinions heard. Women still lag behind in the job-market share, though, and in boardroom participation. Decisions are often made by the male top management only.

Chileans like an introductory session where they get to know each other before discussing business. Typical topics of conversation include family, leisure activities, and Chilean wines. Personal details are not considered off-limits in business conversations.

www.bcentral.cl/eng/index.htm

The role of the Central Bank is to ensure the stability of the national currency, regulate monetary supply, set interest rates, and oversee the commercial banking system (private banks). This website has a great deal of information, including statistics, policies, and historical and current events.

www.foreigninvestment.cl/

The Foreign Investment Committee is the official Chilean agency in charge of promoting foreign investments in the country. Its website provides abundant data and information on Chile's business culture and investment opportunities.

http://data.worldbank.org/country/chile

The World Bank provides financial and technical assistance to developing countries around the globe. They offer low-interest loans, interest-free credits, and grants for projects involved in education, health, agriculture, infrastructure, economic development, and the environment. This website posts economic indicators for Chile. A further search reveals over 400 specific indicators related to development. Much more information can be found by going to the World Bank home page, clicking on "countries" and then on "Chile." This page leads to more statistics and articles on Chile.

**www.iadb.org/research/LatinMacroWatch/CountryTable.
cfm?country=Chile&lang=en**

The Inter-American Development Bank is an international development organization that lends money to countries in Latin America and the Caribbean to finance projects aimed at reducing poverty and inequality. This website provides the latest data on Chile's economic activity and employment. By plugging the word "Chile" into the search function, a student will find information on the national strategy and on ongoing research projects in Chile

ENVIRONMENT

The beautifully rugged landscape of the Atacama Desert.

5

CHILE IS RICH IN natural resources and derives much of its wealth from the land. The northern region, characterized by the rugged beauty of the desert, has vast mineral deposits. The Central Valley is a bountiful source of fruit, vegetables, and wine. The southern region, lush with forests, lakes, and volcanoes, earns its livelihood from the forestry, dairy, and paper industries. The long Pacific coastline harbors fish and shellfish.

As with most modern economies, Chile struggles to maintain a balance between environmental protection and economic growth.

The marshland of the Lago El Toro in Huerquehue National Park is bordered by steep araucaria-covered hills and backed by the snow-sprinkled Cerro Araucario.

The beautiful Andean flamingo species is restricted to the high Andes. It is at risk of extinction because of hunting, its long breeding cycle, and decreasing number of breeding sites around the region.

The Chilean economy depends heavily on its natural resources, but as a developing country, Chile has often not devoted enough attention to environmental causes. As a result, pollution reached dangerous levels, biodiversity decreased, and marine resources dwindled. Only in the 1990s, after sustained economic growth, did the government begin to take major steps to prevent further harm to the environment. Eighteen percent of Chilean territory has been converted to national parks, and pollution-cutting measures have been implemented. Progress has been slow, but Chileans are starting to demand results.

In 2010 the Bachelet government created the Ministry of the Environment, the Service for Environmental Evaluation, and the Superintendency for the Environment, partly in response to requirements to join the OECD (Organization for Economic Cooperation and Development). The new ministry is responsible for developing environmental policy, regulation, and the conservation of biodiversity, water, and renewable resources.

BIOLOGICAL DIVERSITY

In spite of the length of the country and the variety of climates and altitudes, Chile's biodiversity is one of the lowest in all of South America. Chile is home to some 30,000 different animal species. Certain groups are of great importance. For example, about half of the world's species of cetaceans (marine mammals that include whales and dolphins) live in or travel through Chilean waters. Moreover, 20 percent of the world's species of fungi are found in Chile. It is believed that there are many more species yet to be found.

A number of birds are on the endangered list, including the Chilean and Andean flamingos, the condor, the Humboldt and Magellanic penguins, and the brown pelican. About 30 mammals are on the endangered list and include the *huemul* (a deer), the southern river otter, the vicuña (a relative of the llama), and the long-tailed chinchilla. In terms of fish, there are a variety of skates, sharks, and rays on the endangered list as well. The *pudu* (a small deer) and the Magellanic woodpecker are on the verge of extinction. The *toromiro* tree from Easter Island is now extinct in the wild. Some *toromiros* still exist in a handful of botanical gardens around the world, but they are unable to reproduce on their own. The conservation of this rare tree is carried out in a laboratory.

A vicuña with her calf in the cold Altiplano of the Andes Mountains. Their wool is one of the finest and most expensive of natural fibers. During the times of the Inca, only kings and high ranking officials could use this fiber for clothing.

The World Wildlife Foundation has named the island of Chiloé in the south one of 25 priority regions in the world for conservation. This island alone is home to many rare and endangered birds, amphibians, mammals, and freshwater fish. In 2002 CONAMA (the National Commission for the Environment and the predecessor of the Ministry of the Environment) began implementing Regional Strategies for Biodiversity, primarily by creating protected areas, both on land and in marine areas off the long coast.

WATER

Although just about every Chilean has access to clean drinking water, there are real problems with the disposal of wastewater from homes, factories, mines, and agricultural areas, which have high levels of pesticides. Sewage systems are very expensive, so for many years, waste was dumped directly into rivers and the Pacific Ocean. The first law addressing this issue was passed in 1916. The law stated that industries could not dump their waste into water systems without purifying or neutralizing it. The law was ambiguous, however, and poorly enforced. It wasn't until 1993 that a new, more detailed law was

Fishing boats anchored in Lota Harbor.

enacted. This law was modified in 1997, and specific emissions standards were issued in 1998. Chile has also signed a number of international agreements on the issue. Almost all of the country's water treatment plants were built during the 1990s as a result of these actions.

Until very recently in Santiago, waste water was flushed directly into the Mapocho River, which runs through the heart of the city, making the river dirty and smelly. Work began in 2009 on an 18-mile (28.5-km) project to build a tunnel system, running parallel to the river, to deliver the raw sewage to a water treatment plant, thereby cleaning up the river. Other projects under consideration include the possibility of using bacteria to treat mining waste.

The Bío-Bío River, famous among white-water rafters for its rapids, has already been dammed to provide hydroelectric power to meet Chile's growing energy needs.

MARINE RESOURCES

The fishing industry is a key part of the Chilean economy. Chile exports many types of fish and exotic seafood, and it is the world's largest supplier of fish meal. Many species have been overharvested, though, and fish populations have dropped. Also, bottom trawling has damaged the ocean floor. In 2006 Chile joined with other countries in the process to establish the South Pacific Regional Fisheries Management Organization, which aims to manage fisheries resources in a sustainable manner. There has been a noticeable drop in the size of fish catches, especially in the harvest of jurel, or southern jack mackerel, used primarily in fish meal. In 2011 catches fell far short of expectations, and scientists recommended reducing the catch by half in order to let the stock replenish. The number of *locos*, a type of abalone, dropped to such critical levels that it became illegal to harvest or sell them at all. The *locos* made a comeback, however, and can once again be harvested, although within strict limits. Fishing laws have been criticized for their inability to effectively protect Chile's marine species. More attention is needed to policing areas where the fish spawn and grow. Most government-protected areas are land, not bodies of water.

Humboldt penguins, found along the Pacific coast of northern Chile and Peru, have suffered a decline in their population because their food sources have been overfished. Sometimes the penguins become trapped in fishing nets.

Salmon is one of Chile's main exports. Salmon are raised on fish farms, and although this prevents overfishing, it can also have very negative consequences. Fish farms are usually subject to overcrowding, making the use of medications and pesticides a necessity. Excess feed and waste from the farms also contaminate the surrounding area. The infectious salmon anemia virus caused many salmon farms to close in 2008, although it has been reported that improper disposal of the infected fish allowed the virus to enter the ecosystem. Many of these fish farms simply moved to new, uncontaminated areas. Moreover, other wildlife, such as the American sea lion, can become caught in the nets surrounding the farms, leading to suffocation and death. Conservationists assert that laws governing fish farms are not strict enough.

Chile is an original member of the International Whaling Commission (IWC), which was founded in 1946. In 2008 President Michelle Bachelet created a Chilean whale sanctuary and, during a meeting of the IWC, symbolically held at a former whaling factory (closed since 1967) in the town of Quintay, declared a perpetual ban on whaling in Chilean waters.

Salmon fish farms in the Reloncavi Fiord in southern Chile provide a valuable export product.

> ## ORGANIC FARMING

Organic farming has only recently been explored in Chile and remains a small industry. Farmers who first entered this market had a high learning curve and succeeded only through much trial and error, experimenting with different growing methods and different crops. Now there is a government certification system and farmer organizations that let farmers share their experiences with each other. Given its natural barriers and clean water from the Andes Mountains, the geography of Chile helps with organic farming. Most organic products are sold for export and include apples, raspberries, kiwi, avocado, and asparagus. Some wines are also made from organic grapes. Locally there is still little demand for organic products because of a lack of knowledge and an unwillingness to pay more for what looks like the same product. Also, the organic market is in competition with "green" or "healthy" products that are not 100 percent organic.

LAND USE

Only a small proportion of Chile's land is suitable for agriculture. The country has suffered from land erosion for more than 100 years owing to natural causes, such as hilly landscapes, and man-inflicted causes, such as continual animal grazing, poor farming techniques, and urbanization. Desertification affects about 60 percent of Chilean national territory, primarily in the north and south, leading to poverty and high rates of migration. In 1997 Chile joined the United Nations Convention to Combat Desertification. The National Forestry Service (CONAF) coordinates its implementation in Chile through the National Action Plan to Combat Desertification.

Another problem is the use of pesticides in agriculture. While the really bad pesticides have been banned, there are over 900 registered pesticides that can still be used in Chile. Since Chile is a major exporter of fruits and vegetables, growers must abide by the strict oversight required by the various importing countries. Problems also arise from the way pesticides are used. Farm workers tend not to wear the necessary protective gear and so are exposed to the pesticides for longer periods of time than is recommended.

Paving all the streets in Santiago would help to reduce dust and pollution in the city, although average temperatures would rise as a result.

Regrettably, the government's own oversight agency does not have enough resources to fully enforce the laws.

Most Chileans cast out their garbage without a thought as to where it goes or what happens to it. Municipal recycling areas have started to appear in upper middle-class neighborhoods in Santiago, however, where residents can take their paper, plastic bottles, and glass. A change in attitudes will be slow and most likely will depend upon the younger generation's sensibilities. Traditionally, anything that could be sold for reuse, such as paper, cardboard, glass, or metal was collected by *cartoneros* (kahr-toh-NEH-rohs), people who scour the streets, rummaging through the garbage as a way of earning money.

The Bosque Encantado (the Enchanted Forest) in Patagonia.

SAVING THE FORESTS

Chile is blessed with abundant forests, primarily in the south. It is home to the only temperate rain forest in South America, the Valdivian rain forest. These forests are slowly being replaced by tree plantations. In fact, the Maule and Bío-Bío regions already have more plantations than forests. Areas of land are cleared of natural vegetation, and then the seeds of the *radiata* pine tree are sown; this tree grows far more quickly in Chile than in other parts of the world. The logged trees are used to make pulp, cellulose, paper products, and furniture. The whole venture may be a success economically, but it causes soil erosion and the sacrifice of habitat for various species of plants and animals. Eucalyptus trees are not native to Chile, but since their introduction, they too can be seen in many areas due to their quick growth. Forests on the Juan Fernandez Archipelago are threatened as well.

Chile is home to two ancient trees, the alerce and the monkey puzzle tree. The alerce, a larch that is similar to a redwood, grows to over 377 feet (115 m) tall and can live for over 3,000 years. This tree is found in the south and because of its moisture-resistant properties was used extensively in building houses. Many trees were lost; but because of their very slow growth, they could not be easily replaced. The monkey puzzle tree, also known as the araucaria (ar-rauh-KARH-ee-ah), is a conifer that grows to 164 feet (50 m) tall and is the national tree. It may live for over 1,000 years and is easily recognizable by its umbrella shape with distinctive branches.

CONAF oversees the Working Group for Managing a Sustainable Forest, a body made up of conservationists, industrialists, academics, and government officials. The goal of this group is to build agreements on how to best use Chile's forests. The Food and Agriculture Organization of the United Nations (FAO) reported in 2011 that Chile is one of the few countries in the region to have reversed the trend of deforestation. Between 2000 and 2010 FAO found that the amount of land covered by forest increased on average by 98,840 acres (40,000 hectares) per year. Many of the protected forests are in areas with small populations or in inaccessible areas. Nevertheless, attitudes are changing. According to a survey by the Nature Conservancy, almost 60 percent of voters agree that protecting the natural environment should be a priority, even though it might cause some job and investment losses in the short run.

SAVING THE AIR

The most obvious environmental problem in Chile is air pollution, particularly in the big cities. Santiago lies in a valley, and a phenomenon called thermal inversion, affecting the circulation of wind, traps polluted air in the valley. As a result, a dark cloud covers the entire city, especially in winter. When the rains come, the air is cleaned, and the skies are blue. But after a few days, the polluted cloud returns. This smog is the cause of many health problems, primarily respiratory illnesses, especially among the young and the elderly.

Most of the pollution is caused by human activities. It is now illegal to burn firewood in Santiago, which used to be a popular source of heat in the winter—and a big polluter. The biggest sources of pollution are vehicle and factory emissions, dust, and fires. The government has put in place a number

ENVIRONMENTAL ACTIVISM

A civil society, where people are free to form or move within various independent institutions, is becoming more prevalent in Chile, especially those that support environmental causes, and the following are among the better-known examples. Representatives of the Mapuche people have been protesting in the south, near Temuco, claiming that large farms and logging operations in the area infringe on their traditional land. Some of their grievances have turned violent and are part of a larger protest for Mapuche rights. Farther south, in Patagonia, an energy company wants to build hydroelectric dams, which would alter the landscape irreversibly, and then send the electricity all the way to Santiago in a long clear-cut corridor. When the project was approved, sizable demonstrations were held in Santiago and in other parts of the country. There has been a concerted campaign against these plans, with well-organized international participants. Surfers, fishermen, and those involved in the tourism industry came together in the seaside town of Pichilemu to form the Save the Waves Coalition. After two years, this group was successful in blocking plans to build a waste pipeline that would have dumped sewage near the town's main beach, one of the country's best surfing spots. The possible impact on glaciers and the water cycle of high-altitude mining, the construction of new coal-fired power plants, and the presence of toxic substances in populated areas near copper refineries have also created significant citizen response.

of measures to help correct the situation. First, a law was passed requiring each new car purchased to be equipped with a catalytic converter to help reduce emissions. There is also a program called Restricción (rehs-treek-see-OHN), which restricts cars without catalytic converters from driving one day a week between March and December based on the last digit of their license plate. On days with extremely high pollution levels, cars with catalytic converters are also included in the program.

The public transit system in Santiago was revamped in 2007. Part of the plan prohibited the use of old buses. The introduction of new buses with lower emissions significantly reduced the amount of air pollution in the capital.

To help cut factory emissions, no new industries are allowed to start operations in the Santiago metropolitan area. Moreover, some existing industries have been forced to shut down part or all of their operations. Because this can be quite expensive, many factories have moved away from Santiago. The Ministry of the Environment has set up a national program called Clean Air, which uses various strategies, including cash incentives, to control emissions and find a way to monitor air quality.

The city of Santiago lies under a thick cloud of smog for most of the year, largely caused by the discharges of local industries and the growing number of cars in the Chilean capital.

Mining and its related activities are another important source not only of air pollution but of land and water pollution as well. Even though laws have been passed and stricter operating standards are being enforced, there is still plenty of room for improvement.

NEW FORMS OF ENERGY

Energy is needed for economic growth, and one of Chile's imminent problems is insufficient energy resources. New forms of energy, such as solar, wind, and tidal, are being explored. In fact, wind farms have been built in both the north and the south. Experimental efforts are under way to transform seaweed into biofuel. Significant advances must be made, however, to render these sources of energy feasible and cost-effective.

INTERNET LINKS

www.nature.org/wherewework/southamerica/chile/

This Nature Conservancy website provides information on the various natural habitats of Chile, strategies for protecting them, and community involvement. It also has a lot of information on specific local initiatives.

www.worldwildlife.org/what/wherewework/southernchile/index.html

This article, entitled "A Land of Ancient Forests and Abundant Oceans," touches on the species that are in most need of protection and on local communities. There are many other articles on Chile in this website, which can be found by searching for "Chile."

www.greenpeace.org/international/en/system-templates/search-results/?all=chile

Greenpeace is an active environmental protection organization. This website provides several different articles on various environmental issues regarding Chile.

CHILEANS

A farmer and his son relaxing on their farm in the Central Valley of Chile.

6

Chileans have a strong national identity and play down regional differences. In spite of the distances between the north and the far south, Chileans are one people.

C LOSE TO 17 MILLION people make up the Chilean population. Most Chileans have both European (primarily Spanish) and indigenous blood. There are also small groups of Chileans of Arab and Asian descent. A significant group of Chileans are indigenous, mostly Mapuche and Aymara. The people of Easter Island are Polynesian.

Even though most Chileans have some indigenous blood, they are sensitive about the subject of mixed ethnicity. In general, Chileans see themselves as Caucasians and are more greatly influenced by European and North American cultures than by historic indigenous cultures.

Chileans are not as ethnically diverse as other Latin Americans. In fact, Chile is said to be one of the most homogeneous countries in South America. Immigrants did not settle in Chile in great numbers the way they did in Brazil and Argentina, and Chile's unique, protected geography has kept it naturally isolated from the rest of the world.

Small groups of German, French, Italian, and Swiss immigrants did come to Chile in the mid-1800s. People from England, Ireland, Croatia, Palestine, and Korea immigrated in later years. Some typical non-Spanish Chilean surnames are Edwards, Lyon, Schmidt, Newman, Yerkovic, and Ross.

Central Chile has only 18 percent of the nation's land, but about 80 percent of its people. Today, around 88 percent of Chileans live in urban areas, compared with only 68 percent in 1960 and 20 percent a hundred years ago. Just over 40 percent of all Chileans reside in Santiago, the capital. Other populous cities are Valparaíso-Viña del Mar

and Concepción in central Chile, Temuco in southern Chile, and Antofagasta near the Atacama Desert. Many German immigrants settled in the southern cities of Valdivia, Llanquihue, and Osorno. Many Croatians have made their homes in Punta Arenas and Tierra del Fuego in the south and Antofagasta in the north. The Mapuche Indians live mainly in the southern Central Valley near the city of Temuco. The Aymara Indians live in the far north near the borders of Bolivia and Peru, and the Rapa Nui Polynesians live on Easter Island.

The fertility rate in Chile is 15 births per 1,000 people and population growth averages 1 percent per year. The infant mortality rate is comparatively low at around 7 out of every 1,000 live births and has been dropping. The average life expectancy is 78 years. Major causes of death are heart disease and cancer.

Young Polynesians on Easter Island (Rapa Nui) showing their body paintings in the style of their ancestors during ceremonial dances.

INDIGENOUS POPULATIONS

Prior to the arrival of the Spanish adventurers, the indigenous population was never particularly large or concentrated in any one area. The Aymara, Atacameño, and Diaguita peoples lived in the Atacama region; the Mapuche in the Central Valley and on Chiloé Island; and the Chonos, Kawesqar, Selk'nam, and Yagan peoples in the far south. Many of these groups did not survive the presence of Europeans, as the Spanish conquest brought with it slavery, war, and fatal diseases such as smallpox.

Only a relatively small indigenous population remains today. Entire ethnic groups, including the Ona or Selk'nam, Yagan, and Diaguita, have been completely wiped out. The largest indigenous group in Chile, the Mapuche, stands today at somewhat over 600,000. The Mapuche fought the European settlers well into the late 19th century. They were the only native people in North and South America to effectively resist the Spanish during the entire colonial period. It is said that the Mapuche never really surrendered; they simply stopped fighting, which they had done supremely well.

The Spaniard Pedro de Valdivia described the Mapuche as a strong, handsome, and friendly people. Other colonists wrote of their serious manner, their ability to withstand severe hardship, and their intimacy with the land they farmed. They did not build temples; they believed in magic and omens sent by trees, birds, or the wind. The women were said to be beautiful in their brightly colored clothing, jewelry, and headdresses. The men were fierce and clever warriors.

Mapuche means "people of the land," and members of the group feel passionately about the loss of their territory. They separate themselves from outsiders, whom they call *huincas* (oo-EEN-kahs) or just Chileans.

The Mapuche are a tight-knit community. They speak Spanish, but they also have their own language, called Mapudungun. Many think that the government has treated them unfairly, that their ancestral rights have been violated, and their lands confiscated. There have been consistent, and sometimes violent, actions in the south against the government and local landowners. Some Mapuche protesters who clashed with police were arrested and charged under Chile's strict antiterrorism law. The prisoners went on a hunger strike in 2010 arguing that their trial was unfair and the sentences too harsh, at the same time demanding the return of their ancestral lands. The government agreed to drop the terrorism charges and charged them instead with common crimes in October 2010. In early 2011 there was another hunger strike that lasted 86 days, once again in opposition of the application of Chile's antiterrorism law.

Generally, the Mapuche are impoverished and have inadequate medical care and few opportunities for advancement, in spite of governmental efforts to reverse the intolerable situation. Most Mapuche live south of the Bío-Bío River. Many have migrated to large cities such as Santiago and Concepción—most often because of economic hardship or the search for better education or work opportunities. It used to be rare to find anyone with a Mapuche surname in a professional position, but that is beginning to change. Pride in the Mapuche heritage is alive and growing.

Mapuche women standing with traditional rhythm instruments in front of their home in Temuco.

THE FIRST CHILEANS

Spanish colonists arrived in the mid-16th century, and because originally only men came from Spain, they married local indigenous women. Spaniards continued to immigrate and eventually women joined the men. Recent arrivals were known as *peninsulares* (pe-nihn-su-LAHR-ays), while the term criollos was used to describe Spaniards born on Chilean soil. In the late 18th and early 19th centuries, Basques from the Pyrenees began to arrive in Chile in significant numbers. They soon took jobs as merchants and traders and bought up large pieces of land. After two or three generations, they were firmly ensconced in the upper class. Some of the largest vineyards today are owned by families of Basque heritage, as evidenced by the names on the wine labels. English, Irish, and Scottish immigrants followed. The British settled in Valparaíso and were instrumental in the formation and development of the Chilean navy.

In the mid-1800s thousands of Germans migrated to Chile as part of a program to populate the country south of the Bío-Bío River. They found the climate similar to that of their German homeland and thus set up homes and became farmers. Now, many Germans in Chile raise cattle for milk and grow crops, such as potatoes, beets, and oats. Hotels and pastry shops with German names are common in this area of the country.

During the height of European immigration, between 1883 and 1901, only 36,000 Europeans came to Chile. (More newcomers migrated to the United States in a single month during the same period.) Although their numbers were small, the immigrants made a significant impact on Chilean society. They had been members of the educated middle class in their home countries and brought much-needed job skills to their new land.

Some 25,000 Croatians migrated to Chile in the late 19th century to take their chances in the gold rush in Tierra del Fuego. From there, many became successful fishermen, merchants, and shipbuilders. Today,

Descendants of Chile's immigrant population drive an ox cart down a country road.

many Chilean Slavic descendants are professionals, governmental employees, and businessmen. The 20th century saw new waves of immigrants, such as Christian Palestinians. Most of them established small businesses, especially in textile manufacturing, that later became quite successful. Jews who came from Europe and the Middle East moved to urban areas and started retail businesses. Koreans made up the next wave of immigrants, and many moved into the textile businesses formerly run by the Palestinians. In the 21st century there has been a tidal wave of immigration from other Latin American countries, especially Peru. As the Chilean economy grew while nearby countries struggled, many hopeful families saw Chile as the land of opportunity.

As many as 1 million Chileans, mostly professionals, intellectuals, and artists, were exiled to other Latin American countries, Europe, North America, and Australia during the harsh period of the military (Pinochet) government. Following the return to democracy, many Chileans, called *retornados* (the returned), chose to come back to their homeland.

CLASS STRUCTURE

From a class structure point of view, Chilean society resembles a pyramid: the small upper class is at the top, the middle class forms the center, and the lower class is at the bottom. The three classes have vastly different experiences, ways of life, and income levels. An area of concern is the growing gap between the wealthy and the poor. Even though a successful economy means better opportunities for everyone, the top 10 percent of the population still controls 40 percent of the nation's wealth and the poorest 10 percent controls a meager 0.9 percent.

THE UPPER CLASS As in most countries, there is a sector of Chilean society that has held power and wealth for generations. These families, whose wealth was based on landownership, are well known and easily maintain their positions. There is also social mobility, however, and with the surge in the economy, a nouveau riche sector has emerged. This new group of upper-class people has made its fortune in industry and business.

Unlike other Latin American countries whose rural economies during the colonial era were based on labor-intensive crops, Chile did not import a large number of slaves from Africa.

Chileans of all ages and classes come together to enjoy a peaceful day in the Plaza de Armas park in downtown Santiago.

Members of the upper-class are well educated, and their children go to exclusive private schools. They will go on to attend one of the traditional universities, probably the University of Chile or Catholic University, or the best private colleges, and may pursue master's degrees or doctorates in the United States or Europe. They have access to very high-quality private health care.

Upper class families have large comfortable homes in the city and either a beach or a country home. They purchase designer goods and many travel abroad quite often. Nevertheless, Chileans generally tend to be modest and avoid showy behavior.

THE MIDDLE CLASS A hundred years ago, the middle class was made up of only a small group of merchants and small-scale businessmen. The discovery of nitrates and then copper provided significant employment opportunities for Chileans and set the stage for the country's modern labor force. Today, the middle class makes up the heart of the country. Many work in commerce, government, service industries, and in manufacturing.

By and large, they are well educated and family-oriented people. They either own or rent a medium- to small-size house or apartment. Knowing that education is very important, many families consider that sending their children to private schools is a high priority. They vacation primarily within Chile and will always find time to visit their beloved beaches in the summer.

THE LOWER CLASS This class includes urban laborers, factory workers, domestics, small farmers, sharecroppers, and copper and coal miners, as well as the many unemployed city dwellers. Lower-class families are close and traditionally provide help to any member of the family needing it.

Households are often made up of kinfolk from several generations, many of whom need to work to help keep food on the table for the entire family.

Their children attend public schools, often of regrettably low quality. They use the public health-care system that, due to reduced funding, depends upon older and lower quality facilities. The poor are more likely to be victims of crimes and run an increased risk of drug and alcohol abuse.

DRESS STYLES

Chileans dress much like North Americans, although never as informally as the most casual Americans. Sneakers are reserved for exercising and only young people wear them on the street. Nor will adult Chileans wear shorts, except at the beach. Women tend to look very put together when out shopping, and high heels are not uncommon for everyday use. Men wear suits and ties to work and, with the exception of trendy or foreign-owned companies, there is no such thing as casual dress days. In some places, such as banks or government agencies, the secretaries wear uniforms.

Young *huasos*, dressed in their traditional colorful outfits, taking part in a regional rodeo competition.

All school children wear uniforms, regardless of whether they attend public or private schools. There might be slight differences, but in general girls wear white blouses and navy blue skirts or jumpers, and boys wear gray slacks and white shirts with navy blue sweaters or blazers.

The most traditional Chilean outfit is that worn by the *huaso* (WAH-soh), or horseman, normally during a festival or rodeo. *Huasos* wear a flat-brimmed, flat-topped hat that originated in the Andalusian region of southern Spain and a bolero jacket covered by a manta or a colorful cloak. The manta, often multicolored, is known for its intricate design, creative patterns and fine craftsmanship.

Huasos frequently wear black pinstriped pants, leather leggings, and short, pointed high-heeled boots with spurs. In the 18th century Chilean spurs were

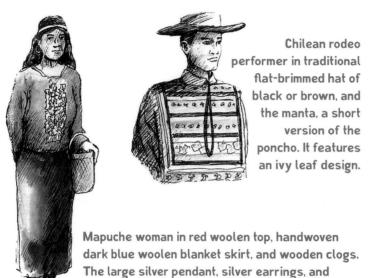

Chilean rodeo performer in traditional flat-brimmed hat of black or brown, and the manta, a short version of the poncho. It features an ivy leaf design.

Cowboy (huaso) in light brown woolen poncho and dark blue corduroy breeches. Leather boots, a belt, and a gray felt hat add the finishing touches.

Mapuche woman in red woolen top, handwoven dark blue woolen blanket skirt, and wooden clogs. The large silver pendant, silver earrings, and headpiece show the influence of Incan culture.

Chilean rancher in handwoven woolen poncho and a straw sombrero, leather boots, and decorative spurs. The spurs are not used to rake the horse's flesh but are pressed flat against the animal's sides. The saddle consists of several layers of felt.

Mapuche man on horseback. Beneath the woolen blanket poncho he wears a shirt and trousers of llama wool simply wrapped around the legs and pulled up under the belt. A black felt hat protects his head. A superb horseman, he has no need for such extras as boots, stirrups, or spurs. A felt saddle and a simple loop for the big toe are sufficient.

known for their size and decorative quality. They were about 6 inches (15 cm) across and had up to 24 points. Today, the typical spur is only 3 or 4 inches (8 or 10 cm) across.

Besides central Chile, other regions have their own traditional dress. For example, the Aymara women are known for their bowler hats and colorful big skirts, similar to the ones worn by Aymara women in Bolivia.

INTERNET LINKS

www.thisischile.cl/frmContenidos.aspx?ID=1206&sec=357&eje=Acerca&itz=interface-acerca-gente-gente

This government website offers a great deal of information about the people of Chile and examines such topics as ethnic groups, religion, language, immigration, and Chileans abroad.

www.cholchol.org/en_mapuche.php

The Chol-Chol Foundation is a highly respected nonprofit, fair-trade, nongovernment organization dedicated to helping the Mapuche people. This page provides information on Mapuche history and culture.

www.everyculture.com/Bo-Co/Chile.html

This detailed website provides information on cultural and national identity and demographics. It covers the presence of diverse ethnic groups in Chile and the different social strata comprising Chilean society. It also reports on additional topics, such as history, government, and national symbols.

www.polynesia.com/rapa-nui/island-map.html

This site provides an abundance of information on the Polynesian people of Rapa Nui, or Easter Island. Among other topics, it describes the people, the *moais*—the famed carved stone figures—and the island's geography, language, and history.

In recent years Chile has seen a surge in the number of temporary expatriates living in Santiago and other major cities. Not only do many international firms have offices in the country, Chile is also a major destination for university study-abroad programs.

LIFESTYLE

Chileans shopping at a mall in Santiago.

C HILE IS A WESTERN SOCIETY, and therefore, daily life does not differ much from that experienced in North America or Europe. As in any society, however, one's Chilean lifestyle varies dramatically based on who you are, what you do, and where you live.

Life in Chile centers around the main pillars of work, study, family, and leisure. People spend many hours at the office or studying in an effort to get ahead. Social occasions often revolve around the family, which is of the utmost importance. Free time is often enjoyed with family or a circle of long-time close friends. The home is thought of as a very special place. Chileans open up their doors to foreigners, and guests are made to feel like family members.

Friends catching up over a meal at the Central Market (Mercado Central) in Santiago.

LIFE IN SANTIAGO

Just over 40 percent of all Chileans live in Santiago, the seventh-largest city in Latin America. Santiago is the home of both the wealthiest and some of the poorest in Chilean society. Santiago is the cultural and intellectual hub of the country, the place where trends are set and where things are happening. The city center is the location of government buildings, shops, and offices. Moreover, with the construction of new apartment buildings, downtown Santiago is again becoming a popular place to live. Trendy new residential and corporate areas have emerged in some of the suburbs. Many businesses have moved their offices to these stylish areas that also boast fine restaurants, stores, and apartment buildings. During rush hour traffic congestion is serious, and in the winter, the smog becomes a major suffocating problem.

In the late 18th century Santiago had a small population of around 30,000. Nearly 90 percent of Chileans lived on farms in the countryside. By the mid-19th century, the city had grown to 150,000 inhabitants, good roads and railways had been built, and the colonial aristocracy had settled in. The rise in population was due to mass migration from the countryside, which continued well into the 20th century.

Commuters traveling on the underground Metro at a station in Santiago.

HOUSING

Originally, such migrants were forced to live in slums or tenements. Then they began to build makeshift homes on the unused land just outside the city. These came to be known as *poblaciones callampas* (poh-blah-see-OH-ness kah-YAHM-pahs), or mushroom villages. The dwellings were usually put together flimsily from cardboard and tin. Few had running water, but many had electricity illegally siphoned off from power lines. Water came from a common faucet.

Beginning in the 1960s the government made efforts to improve the living conditions in the *callampas* or to move the inhabitants to better housing. Important advances were made by President Eduardo Frei Montalva in the mid-1960s. The Pinochet government initiated massive low-income housing programs, ranging from small apartments in four-story buildings to houses and plots of land with only the most basic facilities. These housing projects were improved by the democratic governments that followed, but overcrowding, poor safety, and a lack of social facilities continue to beset the residents. Serious flooding is a major issue every winter when the rains begin.

In 1997 Un Techo Para Chile (A Roof for Chile) was founded. The goal of this philanthropic organization is to eradicate slums by building housing for the neediest sectors. Over the years more than 100,000 young volunteers have worked to build over 50,000 homes. Since 2001 the organization has expanded into 19 Latin American countries.

Santiago's upper class lives in large and comfortable apartments or homes in the so-called *barrio alto* (BAH-ree-oh AHL-toh), the upper-class neighborhood. Some of these homes are modern, others are in the colonial style, complete with courtyards and tiled roofs. Many have gardens and

Homes on the steep Cerro Alegre hillside in Valparaíso.

A *ruca*, the traditional Mapuche Indian house in Temuco.

terraces with pools that provide spectacular views of the city or the nearby Andes mountain range.

Middle-class homes are found in new apartment buildings and small houses. Several large middle-class neighborhoods have risen all across the Santiago metropolitan area over the past 20 years. The traditional Chilean rural house is only one story and has long, dark corridors leading to large rooms with high ceilings and a large kitchen. Stables are nearby. Some grander homes have their own orchards and often a small vineyard. The small farmhouse may have the same elements but on a much reduced scale. Adobe brick is still a common building material.

Although many Mapuche live in modern housing, a few still live in traditional dwellings called *rucas* (ROO-kahs), found primarily on farmland near the city of Temuco. The low walls are wooden, and the roof is thatched and comes to a peak. Inside, there is an earthen floor, often covered with a beautiful handmade rug, and a *fogon* (foh-GOHN), a fire pit that is used for both heating the home and cooking.

LIFE IN THE COUNTRY

The typical rural family in Chile most likely lives and works on a farm, or *fundo*, or in a small town. They may also cultivate a small plot of land known as a *parcela* (pahr-SEL-ah). A *parcela* is usually about 1.2 acres (5,000 square meters). The average farm day begins at dawn, when the family goes to the barn to milk the cows. At about 7 A.M. they sit down to a breakfast of rolls and coffee.

The day will be filled with the many necessary tasks related to cultivating crops and raising animals. Fresh meat and vegetables are normally purchased at a nearby outdoor market. In some cases the farm may be near a major

NANAS

Most Chilean middle-class and practically all upper-class families have a nana *(a maid). Previously, most* nanas *lived in the home and provided all sorts of assistance—food preparation, housecleaning, laundry, child rearing, and so forth. Sundays were their day off. Many of these women came from the countryside and, to a degree, became members of the employer family. As the economy prospered, however, fewer Chilean women sought work as* nanas. *Today, these live-in jobs are being filled primarily by Peruvians and other Latin Americans. Many modern families employ* nanas *on a daily basis, working full days Monday through Friday, or perhaps two or three days per week only. Long hours on the job are common, so many working parents rely on* nanas *to pick the children up after school, feed them dinner, and get them ready for bed. Part-time jobs in Chile are rare, so working mothers must find someone they can depend on.*

city, so the shopping can be done at a supermarket. Other farms may be very isolated, and trips to the local market are less frequent.

Children attend schools similar to the schools in cities, but smaller. The pupils wear the same uniform as their city peers. On Sundays, the family attends Mass together. The meal following the Mass is the most elaborate of the week and is shared with cousins, aunts, uncles, and grandparents. After lunch, the children might go horseback-riding or spend time watching television, reading, or playing soccer or tag.

GENDER ROLES

Like most other Latin American countries, Chile is a male-dominated society. Men are expected to provide financial security for the family. Women have to take care of the home and raise the children, often while working outside the home as well, and they tend to single-handedly run the household.

Chileans customarily wed in their 20s. Once married, a couple will start their family immediately. Middle-class families tend to be small, whereas wealthy and poor families are larger. Men are not likely to help out in domestic

A visitor in Chile might hear someone referred to as the *regalón* (ray-gah-LOHN) of the family. Every family has one. This term means spoiled, but in a positive sense, as in a much-loved child who is pampered. It should not be confused with a spoiled brat.

chores, even if they are unemployed, although some younger men may be more willing to help. At meals, their wives serve them before the rest of the family. Single-parent homes, most often headed by the mother, are becoming very common.

Chilean children have a sense of duty toward their parents and frequently live at home until they marry. When they do leave home, they usually live in the same town or village, come home on Sundays and important holidays, and maintain a close relationship with their parents. Chilean parents tend to be very protective of their children. They exert a great deal of influence and are involved in their children's lives, even when their children have families of their own.

Chilean women from all social classes are often employed outside the home, either by necessity or by choice. They work in many sectors of the economy as teachers, nurses, domestics, office workers, social workers, journalists, economists, business professionals, doctors, and lawyers. Men are often proud of their wives' accomplishments.

Women in Chile have been very active in political activities. During the Allende government women banged pots and pans from their windows to protest spiraling inflation and shortages of basic goods. Women also publicly protested the period of military rule. The mothers, wives, and daughters of the disappeared put pressure on the government to provide information on the whereabouts of their missing family members. For example, a group of women performed the national folk dance, the *cueca* (KWAY-kah), without the required male partner, as a startling way of bringing attention to their missing loved ones.

Even though women, in general, are underrepresented in governmental and leadership positions, Chile was the first South American country to elect a woman president, Dr. Michelle Bachelet, who took office in 2006.

Women demonstrating against domestic violence in Concepción. Women in Chile are politically active and do not hesitate to take on the government when they feel their rights have been abridged.

Like most Latin Americans, Chileans like to take their time about things. In Chile one needs never to apologize for mild tardiness. It is customary to arrive at least 15 minutes late for a small dinner party and up to 30 minutes late for a large party. Once dinner has been finished, Chileans will linger for a long time, chatting. It would be rude to leave immediately following the meal. It is not acceptable, on the other hand, to be late for a business appointment.

At the first meeting with a new client, businesspeople spend a good amount of time in casual conversation before getting down to business. Typical Chileans tend to dislike forwardness and aggressiveness of any kind. They prefer to spend time getting to know someone fairly well before discussing highly personal or sensitive matters.

THE CHILEAN LIFE CYCLE

The important events in the life of a typical Chilean are usually enacted either in the Roman Catholic Church or in the Evangelical Church.

A bride rides in a simple wedding procession on Easter Island.

WEDDINGS Chileans are not given to flashy displays of wealth or status; they tend to celebrate important occasions in a modest, dignified manner. Weddings, for examples, are rarely formal affairs. Chilean brides do not have bridesmaids or attendants to walk before them down the aisle. The bride is escorted only by her father, who hands her to the groom as they reach the altar. During the ceremony, which can be a brief 20-minute service or a full hour-long Mass, the parents of the bride stand next to her and the parents of the groom next to him.

Wedding reception parties are usually held at home or in a small hall, often adjoining the church. Celebratory wine and champagne are served with the wedding dinner. This often consists of a very simple meal of meat, rice, salad, and cake. Usually there is dancing after dinner, with children and the elderly joining in. Afterward, the couple leaves for their honeymoon; popular locations are Viña del Mar, Rio de Janeiro, or Buenos Aires. Members of the upper class hold more elaborate weddings and might go as far as Europe or the United States for their honeymoons.

A church wedding is not a legal ceremony in Chile. So a few weeks prior to the church ceremony couples must marry in a civil ceremony, usually witnessed by only two friends or family. They do not live together, however, until after the church rites.

FUNERALS These also are simple events. The body of the deceased is sometimes kept at home before the religious ceremony, though more often the wake takes place at a church or chapel. During this time friends and relatives visit to provide comfort to the bereaved and to say prayers for the soul of the deceased. Normally there is just a brief memorial church service, followed by a short graveside prayer. Few mourners wear black to funerals in Chile anymore, although traditionally a widow was expected to wear dark clothing for several months after the death of her husband.

Though not often done, a clown livens up the birthday party of this child in Chile.

BIRTHDAYS In Chile children's birthday parties are generally quite modest. Often the event is held at home with a hired clown or puppet show or given at a fast-food restaurant, such as McDonald's or Chuck E. Cheese's, at a video arcade or a sporting venue. As a family's income level rises, the parties tend to become more elaborate. A tradition among children is that after the guests have finished singing "Happy Birthday," they call for the *mordisco* (mohr-DEES-koh) or "big bite." The birthday boy or girl will take a huge bite out of the cake without using their hands, and sometimes their faces are pushed into the cake amid merry laughter.

Schoolchildren in Santiago enjoying their lunch break.

Chilean girls do not have fancy parties to celebrate their 15th birthday (*quincañera*) the way girls do in many other Latin American countries. Adults might celebrate their birthday with a barbecue, karaoke, and dancing.

THE EDUCATIONAL SYSTEM

Chileans are very committed to education, and their educational system, based on French and German models, is highly regarded throughout Latin America. Getting a good education is a priority for the lower and middle classes as they seek to improve their living standards. Many Chilean social activists, the *acriviaras*, are also passionate about providing a good education for all Chileans, regardless of their social class.

There are three types of schools in Chile: public, private (many of which are religious), and privately run but publicly funded (these do not charge their students tuition). Some private Catholic schools have very strict admission guidelines. For example, children of divorced parents are not accepted at certain conservative schools.

In 1880 urban children were given free, compulsory education; in 1920, the same was done for rural children. Now children are required to attend

In 2006 thousands of high school students led massive protests demanding, among other things, higher quality public education and lower costs for students. The students were referred to as pinguinos *(peen-GWEE-nohs), or penguins, because they resembled the birds when wearing their uniforms. Private and public students alike went on strike and hundreds took control of their schools. Wealthy students went on strike in support of poorer students. The strikes ended when the students agreed to participate in an advisory committee that would report to the government. Although some few concessions were granted, deep inequalities still exist in Chilean education, and there is always the threat of more student protests as the struggle to improve education continues.*

The University of Chile in Santiago.

eight years of primary school and can go on to four years of secondary or vocational school. After secondary school, those who qualify can go on to university for degree studies.

The typical primary school curriculum consists of subjects such as arithmetic, Spanish, English, art, science, history, and physical education. The optional secondary school program has two curricula: an arts and sciences program to prepare children headed for college; and a vocational program to teach job skills.

Chile has a very high literacy rate, nearly 99 percent. Close to 90 percent of children finish elementary school and almost 70 percent finish high school.

Overcoming inequalities, improving quality, and increasing affordability are probably the main challenges facing the Chilean educational system today, as well as its being the focus of strong social, political, and ideological debate.

Chile's universities are held in high regard throughout the region. The University of Chile, established in 1738, is the principal university in the country. The private Catholic University in Santiago has been linked to the elite social stratum. There are universities in every major city. The University of Concepción and the University Austral of Valdivia are two well-known schools. There are also a growing number of smaller private universities. Changes in legislation under the military dictatorship allowed private, for-profit universities to open. This has led to a large number of new universities, thereby increasing the numbers of college-educated adults. The traditional universities, meanwhile, continue to enjoy the best reputations.

INTERNET LINKS

www.allsouthernchile.com/chile-relocation-and-retirement-articles/153/641-moving-to-chile.html

This website is for people traveling or moving to Chile. It explains many of the details necessary to function in Chilean society. It is a great resource for the many questions that arise regarding everyday activities in Chile, such as working, studying, dealing with police, health issues, visa regulations, settling into a home or apartment, and finding religious and social groups.

http://genderindex.org/country/chile

This website, maintained by the OECD (Organization for Economic Cooperation and Development) provides useful information on the status of women in present-day Chile. It explores the political and legal rights of women.

www.guardian.co.uk/world/2006/jun/07/chile.schoolsworldwide

This newspaper article recaps the student protests of 2006, when students went on strike seeking lower fees, free bus passes, participation in governmental policy, and better education, especially for the poor, who attend publicly funded schools. The article includes interviews with students. A similar article can be found at http://news.bbc.co.uk/2/hi/americas/5048130.stm, on the BBC.

Many Chileans still smoke cigarettes, although recent laws have attempted to curtail the amount of smoking. Restaurants must have an enclosed dedicated smoking section that is separate from the nonsmoking section and is closed to children. Smoking is forbidden in public buildings.

RELIGION

The exquisite interior of the Cathedral of Santiago. Initially ordered by Pedro de Valdivia in 1541, the church was declared a national monument in 1951.

8

RELIGION IS AN element of Chilean culture that unites the people. Over 70 percent of Chileans identify themselves as Roman Catholic, although a much smaller percentage of them are actually practicing Catholics. About 15 percent are Protestants, most belonging to fundamentalist churches.

The Church of Jesus Christ of Latter-Day Saints, or Mormons, is also a growing presence in Chile. Slightly over 4 percent together are Jewish,

Devotional "thank you" notes, or *gracias*, to the Virgin Mary at the Cathedral of San Marcos in Norte Grande, designed by Gustave Eiffel (of Eiffel Tower fame).

Fresh flowers brighten a cemetery in Putre.

Muslim, Buddhist, or belong to such other faiths as Baha'i. The Mapuche Indians had their own belief system arising from their natural surroundings, and some still observe it. Moreover, 10 percent of the population classifies itself as agnostic.

Fewer than half of nominal Chilean Catholics attend Mass regularly. Those between 11 and 20 years of age attend Mass still less frequently. Nevertheless, many Catholics participate in the sacraments such as First Holy Communion and marriage. Despite low participation in church activities, Chileans still consider themselves to be a Catholic or Christian people.

About one-third of Chilean children attend Catholic schools, where they are immersed in the teachings of the church, as well as strong core subjects.

The Chilean clergy has a history of social concern and progressive thought. Chile's most revered saint, Saint Alberto Hurtado Cruchaga (1901—52), took in homeless children and started the country's most important charity, Hogar de Cristo (House of Christ). He was a Jesuit priest who changed the way people looked at the poor, teaching that they are worthy of respect and compassion. Padre Hurtado was canonized by Pope Benedict XVI on October 23, 2005. He is deeply beloved and admired by a sizable majority of Chileans. Chile's first saint was Santa Teresa de los Andes, who was canonized in 1993. The Catholic Church suffered a setback of popularity in 2011, due to a number of scandals involving priests and illegal or improper behavior.

RELIGION AND SOCIAL CLASS

Historically, the urban upper classes and wealthy landowners had a close relationship with the church, and the two influenced each other. On the other hand, the working poor had neither the time nor the money to learn

ROADSIDE SHRINES

When traveling along any of Chile's highways or rural side roads, a visitor will come across small roadside shrines called animitas *(ah-nee-MEE-tahs), which means "little souls." These shrines are built in memory of a loved one who was killed at that spot, most likely the result of a traffic accident. The shrines are tended to regularly and may be decorated with photos, flowers, candles, and sayings. It is a place for prayer and quiet contemplation. Sometimes the deceased may be called upon to intercede on behalf of a relative in need.*

the teachings of Catholicism through formal education. They often became attached to one or more saints or representations of the Virgin Mary and turned to the church mainly for the important rites of baptism, First Communion, marriage, and burial.

Today, conservative orders of the Catholic Church have a strong presence among very wealthy Chileans. Opus Dei and Legionnaires of Christ run elite schools and oversee prosperous parishes. Meanwhile, the evangelical churches have focused their efforts on the needier sectors of society and work to combat alcoholism, unemployment, and other social problems.

CHURCH AND STATE

The 1925 constitution provided for freedom of religion, giving the Roman Catholic Church independence from the state. In spite of this, the Catholics have been able to exert a level of influence on social policies. For example, due to pressure from the church hierarchy, Chile remained one of the last countries in the world to legalize divorce. The law making divorce possible went into effect only in 2004.

During the military dictatorship a segment of the church publically helped those opposed to Pinochet's rule. In the mid-1970s Cardinal Raúl Silva Henríquez established an organization called the Vicariate of Solidarity, a group of full-time lawyers and volunteers dedicated to defending victims of human rights abuses. The organization also provided counseling and set up workshops for victims and their families.

On November 1, All Saints' Day, Chileans head to the cemetery to pay their respects to loved ones who have died.

Although there is separation of church and state, Chilean presidents had always been practicing Catholics. It is interesting, therefore, to note that President Michelle Bachelet, in addition to her being the country's first woman president, was also the country's first openly agnostic president.

ROMAN CATHOLIC BELIEFS AND TRADITIONS

Roman Catholics believe that the pope is the leader of the church and that his decisions are infallible. Also, Catholics receive a series of sacraments to nourish their spiritual life.

The first sacrament is baptism, when infants are cleansed of their "original sin." In Chile children are baptized when they are about six months old. Parents invite family members and friends to witness the ceremony and to celebrate with them at home after the ceremony. Godparents are appointed before the baptism; they promise to raise the child and oversee his or her religious education in the event of the parents' deaths.

The sacrament of First Communion is the child's introduction to receiving the body and blood of Christ in the form of bread and wine. Chilean children receive their First Communion between second and fourth grades, or between ages 8 and 10, often on the Feast of the Immaculate Conception December 8. They attend religious classes to prepare for their First Communion, which is usually a group ceremony. Girls dress in simple white gowns like little brides, and boys wear suits. After the ceremony, the family gathers at home for a modest celebration. A second pair of godparents is often chosen before the First Communion. Some parents invite their children to make the selection.

Marriage is also a sacrament. A church wedding is a sacred religious event and is separate from the civil marriage ceremony. According to Catholic beliefs, marriage is a spiritual union that allows a couple to have children; the bond cannot be broken.

Established by the Mercedarian religious order who arrived with a discovery expedition to Chile, the Basilica and Cloister of la Merced Church in Santiago was constructed in 1566 and is the burial site of many eminent citizens.

Another sacrament is the Anointing of the Sick. This is a rite of healing that can also be used as spiritual preparation for those who are dying. The priest dabs olive oil—a symbol of light, strength, and life—on the forehead of the sick or dying person and asks for forgiveness of their sins. The application of the holy oil serves two functions: it can help the sick person recover or, in terminal cases, prepare the soul for death.

PROTESTANTS

Christians participating in a service at the Pentecostal Church of Chile in Santiago.

About 15 percent of Chileans are Protestants. These include Lutherans, mostly of German ancestry, Seventh-day Adventists, Baptists, and Methodists.

Pentecostalism, which is a form of Protestantism, is a growing movement in South America, especially in Brazil and Chile. Pentecostals believe in expressing themselves during a church service, aloud or through body movements. Although they tend to be apolitical, Latin American Pentecostals are committed to social reform.

The Pentecostal Methodist Church of Chile, founded in 1947 by Bishop Enrique Chávez Campos, is one of the largest national Pentecostal churches in the world. It organizes a grand thanksgiving service every year in the Evangelical Cathedral of Santiago, which has a seating capacity of some 15,000 people. Evangelical pastors, leaders, and the faithful gather to thank God for the country's independence and for the people's right to congregate in the denomination of their choice. Those in attendance also pray for the country's leaders and public servants. The church is open to communication and cooperation with other churches and religious organizations. The Pentecostal Church of Chile is governed by the general assembly that elects an executive committee of twelve members. In 1997 this annual thanksgiving service was named one of the four official acts of the government to commemorate Chile's independence. The president of the republic always attends this religious service.

The Mapuche believe in mythical animals that can perform extraordinary feats. A beast called a cuero (QUER-roh) is a squid with many pairs of eyes. It seizes swimmers, drags them under the surface, and eats them. The camahueto (kah-mah-WAY-toh) is a huge seahorse that can destroy ships. Magicians ride on camahuetos when they travel. Fear of sorcerers, witches, and devils is commonplace among the Mapuche. Diseases are said to be caused by evil spirits that possess the afflicted person's body or by enemies who cast spells.

THE MAPUCHE TRADITION

The Mapuche have a very deep spirituality, based on their belief that there are positive and negative forces at work in everything. The direction east represents the positive forces, so all Mapuche homes face east. The Mapuche god is called Ngenechen, which means "master of the land" or "lord of the people." He is responsible for controlling nature, creating man and animals, and heading a pantheon of other gods who represent the sun, moon, stars, earth, sea, and thunder. To the Mapuche, the forces of evil, which bring floods, famine, and disease, are embodied in Wekufu, who fought unsuccessfully against Ngenechen to wipe out the ancestors of the Mapuche.

The Mapuche consult a medicine woman or *machi* (MAH-chee) to cure sickness, to save a failing crop, or to receive a blessing. Only the *machi* can make contact with Ngenechen, which she does by entering into a trance.

MYTHS OF CHILOÉ ISLAND

Chiloé Island, a community of fishermen and farmers, is steeped in folkloric traditions, and their religious beliefs combine both Mapuche and Catholic elements. Inhabitants of Chiloé believe in Pincoya, a mythical creature that is half-human, half-fish. This protector of all seas is said to live in Lake Huelde on the island and to dance on the shore when the moon is full. If Pincoya dances facing the hills, the Chiloé fishermen's catch will be good. The Chiloé Islanders also believe in a phantom ship, the *Caleuche*, manned by wizards who lure sailors to come on board, then force them to sail forever.

Chiloé Island is also known for its exquisite churches, some more than 200 years old. Many of them are painted in bright colors to offset the dreary, rainy weather.

INTERNET LINKS

www.vatican.va/news_services/liturgy/saints/ns_lit_doc_20051023_cruchaga_en.html

This website provides information about the Roman Catholic faith and biographies of Chilean saints. This link provides specific information on Saint Alberto (Padre Hurtado), universally admired in Chile.

www.mapa.uchile.cl/artesamapuche/ingles/histor.htm

This page, associated with the University of Chile, explains Mapuche religious beliefs and some of their ceremonies. There are additional pages on the geography, arts, and silver work of the Mapuche.

www.chiloeweb.com/chwb/chiloeisland/english/tem_gen_mitologia.html

This page details the mythology of Chiloé Island. It provides drawings of the mythical beings that dwell on the island and descriptions of their origins, physical attributes, and powers.

Many Chileans receive well wishes on their saint's day, and some may even celebrate with a small family gathering and a cake. According to the Catholic calendar, each saint is honored on a different day, and Chileans celebrate the day of the saint for whom they are named.

LANGUAGE

Spanish culture and language, shared by the majority of Chileans, are preserved and strengthened by a wide range of publications in Spanish.

9

S PANISH IS THE official language of Chile. Virtually everyone in the country speaks it. Chile's somewhat isolated geography and colonial Spanish heritage have contributed to the creation of a homogeneous society with shared customs, values, and a common language.

The Mapuche Indians are the largest group of Chileans with a non-Spanish culture. Although the Mapuche can also speak Spanish, they more often speak their own language, Mapudungun, which is an Araucanian language spoken by more than 500,000 indigenous people

Chilean Spanish is quite distinctive, with many local sayings and idioms and an accent that can be difficult to master.

Enterprising boys selling Spanish language newspapers on the street.

Indigenous words have become part of daily life, especially as names of streets, hills, and neighborhoods. For example, Tobalaba (toh-bah-LAH-bah) is the name of a Mapuche chief and a very important street in Santiago. The majestic Manquehue (mahn-KAY-way) hill overlooking the eastern part of Santiago means "place of the condors." Vitacura (vee-tah-CUHR-ah), a suburb of Santiago, means "large rock." Guata (WAH-tah) means "belly," and pololo (poh-LOH-loh) is the name of a small bug that flutters around people. It has come to refer to a boyfriend, and a polola is a girlfriend.

in Chile and Argentina. The Aymara Indian language is spoken by a small group of people in the north. The inhabitants of Easter Island speak Rapa Nui, a Polynesian language, as well as Spanish.

Chileans who travel extensively, work in international firms, or whose jobs place them in contact with tourists, speak English, but the vast majority of Chileans do not. The government has recently placed an emphasis on improving the teaching of English in schools and has implemented a scholarship program to send students to study English in English-speaking countries. Chileans appreciate foreigners who make an attempt to speak Spanish, no matter how limited their ability with the language may be. Chileans generally love talking to foreigners and prefer stumbling communication to none at all.

Signs for skiers on the slopes of the Osorno volcano. Most language barriers can be overcome with the expressive pictures found on many signboards in Chile.

BASIC CHILEAN PRONUNCIATION

SOUND/LETTER	PRONUNCIATION
f, k, l, m, p, t, y, ch	*as in the English language*
a	**a** *as in* "mark"
e	**a** *as in* "make" *or* **e** *in* "let"
i	**ee** *as in* "meet"
o	**o** *as in* "tot" *or* "lot"
u	**oo** *as in* "toot"
y	**ee** *as in* "meet"
b	*resembles a* **v** *when placed between vowels*
c	**s** *as in* "sink" *when before* **e** *or* **i**; *or like* **k** *in* "kite"
d	*resembles* **th** *when at the end of a word*
g	*like* **ch** *in* "loch" *before* **e** *and* **i**; *or like* **g** *in* "girl"
h	*silent*
j	**wh** *as in* "who"
ll	**y** *as in* "yes"
ñ	**ny** *as in* "canyon"
qu	**k** *as in* "kite"
r	*rolled, especially at the beginning of a word*
rr	*strongly rolled*
s	*often dropped at the end of a word*
v	**b** *as in* "bird"
x	**x** *as in* "taxi"; *or* **s** *as in* "sink" *before a consonant*
z	**s** *as in* "sink"

CHILEAN SPANISH

The Spanish spoken in Chile tends to be uniform, although there are subtle regional differences. As in most cultures, the upper social classes are likely to speak a more refined version of the language.

Spanish in Latin America changes from country to country and region to region, sometimes dramatically. A guagua *(wah-wah) is a baby in Chile, Peru, and Bolivia, but a bus in Cuba. A car is an* auto *(AOW-toh) in Chile, a* coche *(KOH-chay) in Argentina, and a* carro *(KAHR-row) in Mexico and Central America. A kite is a* volantín *(voh-lahn-TEEN) in Chile, a* papalote *(pah-pah-LOH-tay) in Mexico, a* barrilete *(bah-rrih-LEH-tay) in Argentina and Uruguay, and a* cometa *(koh-MEH-tah) in other places.*

The Chilean distinctive accent is not one of the easiest Latin American accents to understand. Chileans tend to relax their consonants and retain the use of vowels. Hence, in Chile, the *s* at the end of a word is often dropped or pronounced like an *h. Las manos* sounds like "lah manoh," and *los hombres* like "loh hombreh." The *d* in the final syllable is often "eaten" as well. *Empanada* usually comes out as "empana'a", while *Pelado* sounds like "pela'o."

Chileans speaking on public phones, although cell phones are increasingly popular.

Whatever their geographic region or social level, Chileans are known for speaking extremely fast. This causes whole sounds or syllables to drop off completely: *hasta luego* (so long) becomes "stalugo," and *mi hija* (my daughter—a term of endearment) becomes "mi'ija." Non-Chileans who speak Castilian, the purist form of Spanish from Spain, may have some difficulty following Chilean Spanish.

A Chilean can pick out another Chilean in a crowd of Spanish-speaking people from different countries just by his or her pronunciation, use of slang, or speech patterns. Chileans tend to use the particle *re* (reh) before certain words that they wish to emphasize. "Of course" might come out sounding like "Rrrrreh-claro!" and "How pretty!" like "Rrrrrreh lindo!" In addition, Chileans love to end words with the suffix *-ito* or *-ita*, which means "little." This explains why a grown woman named Clara might still be called Clarita by a good friend as a term of affection. Chileans often use the Italian word for good-bye, *ciao* (CHOW), instead of the Spanish *adiós* (ah-dee-OHS).

NONVERBAL COMMUNICATION

Chileans gesticulate when they speak, but not in an aggressive or confrontational manner. As with many Latin Americans, Chileans touch one another in a dignified manner when greeting. Women friends kiss each other once on the cheek when they meet. Men friends shake hands; if they are good friends, they will also hug and pat each other on the back. Men and women kiss once on the cheek at social events and shake hands in business situations. At small gatherings it is polite to greet and say good-bye to every guest; just a general "hello" is acceptable at large parties.

Spanish has two forms of the word "you," one formal and one informal. In Chile, you would use the formal form *usted* for anyone you have just met or anyone who is significantly older or in a position of respect (like your boss or a dignitary). It is also used as a term of endearment with children. The informal is *tú*, used familiarly among family, peers, and close friends.

If a Chilean holds his hands up, palms outward and fingers apart, he means someone is stupid. Clenching the fist and raising it to eye level is a communist sign, and standing with both arms raised is a sign of protest.

SPANISH NAMES AND TITLES

Chileans follow the Spanish custom of using double surnames. A man named Carlos Rojas Pérez is addressed as Señor Rojas. Rojas is his father's surname, and Pérez is his mother's maiden name. If he marries a woman named Rosa Montalvo García, she does not change her name but will informally be known as Rosa de Rojas. Their children will take the first surnames of their father and mother. Thus they will have the surname Rojas Montalvo. Men and women are usually addressed as Señor (Mr.) or Señora (Mrs.), respectively, followed by their last names. Women and girls often are addressed by strangers as Señorita (Miss). As a sign of respect, older people and people in positions of power are called by their first name and an honorific, Don (lord, owner, or master) or Doña (lady, mistress), such as Don Carlos or Doña Rosa.

THE *RONGORONGO* TABLETS

The ancient people of Easter Island had their own Polynesian language and a script that resembled Egyptian hieroglyphics. In 1864 a European missionary on the island noticed that many of the locals had wooden boards, called *Rongorongo* tablets, on the walls of their homes. These were covered with small pictures of plants, animals, geometric shapes, and celestial beings

A tablet written in *Rongorongo*, the ancient hieroglyphic script from Easter Island.

that had been carved in rows by using sharp stones. Even at that time, the islanders could not decipher the tablets.

According to legend, the ancient ruler of the Easter Islanders, Hotu Matua, brought the tablets to the island in A.D. 450. There were tablets for hymns, crimes, and historical events. Experts have had little luck deciphering the script on the few tablets that still exist on the island. Some believe that the characters do not represent an alphabet, because there are too many of them, but that they tell some sort of story. Others believe that the pictures are not a script at all, but serve as hints to help people remember important verses.

INTERNET LINKS

www.thisischile.cl/frmContenidos.aspx?SEC=361&ID=1209&eje= acerca

Chile's official website provides ample information on the Spanish spoken in Chile. This page covers unique Chilean expressions. Other pages on this site illuminate the history of Chilean Spanish, the influence of other languages, and Chilean slang.

www.contactchile.cl/en/chile-chilenianisms.php

Contact Chile is a relocation business that helps new arrivals with housing, available classes, internships, volunteerism, tourism, and basic tips on how to live in Chile. This website and the one below provide valuable information on speaking Spanish in Chile. This page details the specifics of Chilean Spanish and has a long list of commonly used Chilean phrases and idioms. It provides the literal meaning and the implied meaning and goes on to use the term in a sentence.

www.joeskitchen.com/chile/culture/slang.htm

This website breaks down the intricacies of Chilean Spanish. It has a lot of additional information and photographs of Chile, too.

Chilean slang words and idioms distinguish them from other Latin Americans. For instance, they often use the phrase *al tiro* when they mean "immediately." The word *cachar* means "to understand," and *fome* means "boring."

ARTS

Statuary at the entrance in front of the Fine Arts Museum in Santiago.

10

C HILEANS HAVE GREAT RESPECT for education and the arts. Santiago, the capital, is the center of cultural expression in the country. It is home to various museums, galleries and institutions, all contributing to the vibrant arts scene of the country.

Included are the Museum of Pre-Columbian Art, which contains ancient Latin American artifacts; the Fine Arts Museum, with its excellent collection of Chilean paintings and sculptures; La Moneda Cultural Center and Gabriela Mistral Cultural Center, both housing international exhibitions; and the Municipal Theater, where Chileans attend their notable Ballet de Santiago, the Philharmonic Orchestra, and the opera.

Great contributions to the arts have been made by Chileans, including poets Pablo Neruda and Gabriela Mistral, the artist Roberto Matta, the pianist Claudio Arrau, the novelist Isabel Allende, and folklorist and visual artist Violeta Parra.

Mano de Desierto or *The Hand of the Desert*, by Chilean sculptor Mario Irarrázabal, stands in the Atacama Desert. It is made with iron and concrete.

There is also the San Francisco Church and Museum, which preserves an impressive collection of colonial religious art and antiques. The Santiago home of Nobel Prize-winning Chilean poet Pablo Neruda, La Chascona, is open to the public, as is Cousiño Palace, an 1871 mansion filled with European antiques and decorations. The suburb of Vitacura supports several highly respected art galleries and is the home of the Fashion Museum.

ARTISTS

The best-known Chilean artist is surrealist painter Roberto Matta, whose work is on display in major art museums all around the world. Other respected artists include painters Samy Benmayor, Bororo, José Balmes, Gonzalo Cienfuegos, Gracia Barrios, and Claudio Bravo; sculptors Marta Colvin, Sergio Castillo, Francisco Gazitúa, and Ivan Daiber; and installation artists Alfredo Jaar and Loty Rosenfeld.

The evocative forms of Roberto Matta's 1957 *Eleven Forms of Doubt* are visual analogies of his inner self.

POETRY

Poetry is a dominant art form in Chile. In the 16th century Spanish poet Alonso de Ercilla y Zúñiga published an epic poem called "La Araucana" about the battles between the Spanish and the Mapuche people. This poem is considered Chile's first major literary work and is widely read and memorized by schoolchildren.

Gabriela Mistral (1889—1957), or *la divina* (the divine) Gabriela, as she is called by Chileans, was born Lucila Godoy Alcayaga in Vicuña in 1889. She was a poor but educated rural schoolteacher. She wrote honest, passionate poetry about her village, children, and the loss of love (her lover killed himself when she was 20). Her first volume of poems was published in 1922. Called *Desolación* (*Desolation*), it was about pain and death. *Ternura* (*Tenderness*), published in 1925, celebrated birth and motherhood. Mistral also wrote about love, religion, nature, and justice.

Mistral's poetry is beautiful, compassionate, and discloses a special love for the common country people. As a result, people of all classes adored her. In 1945 she became the first Latin American to receive a Nobel Prize in literature. The judges honored her "for her lyric poetry, which is inspired by powerful emotions and which has made her name a symbol of the idealistic aspirations of the entire Latin American world." When she died in 1957, the Chilean government declared three days of official mourning.

Poet Pablo Neruda (1904—1973), whose real name was Neftalí Ricardo Reyes Basoalto, received a Nobel Prize in literature in 1971. Neruda's early poems dealt with love and nature. His most famous work is *Twenty Love Poems and a Song of Despair*. He was an advocate of the poor, and his later work was highly political. *Canto General* is Pablo Neruda's 10th book of poems.

The interior of Pablo Neruda's home in Isla Negra with his kitsch collections of glassware and other found objects.

"Little children's feet, blue from the cold, how can they see you and not cover you, dear God!"
—Gabriela Mistral

An affirmed communist, Neruda was a friend and ally of President Salvador Allende. He served as Chilean ambassador to France during the Allende government. He composed verse about poverty, hunger, and the plight of the factory worker. Neruda died just weeks after Pinochet came to power and later became a symbol of the artistic freedoms that were crushed under the new totalitarian regime. Chileans and tourists alike flock to the village of Isla Negra to visit his home on the cliffs overlooking the Pacific Ocean. He was a great collector, and this house has his collections of ship mastheads, seashells, and colored glass. His home nestled in the hills of Valparaíso, La Sebastiana, is also a popular museum.

NOVELISTS

Chile's contribution to the celebrated Latin American "Boom," the highly creative and productive period in literature that began in the 1960s and flourished for two decades, was led by authors José Donoso and Jorge Edwards.

Jorge Edwards was trained as a lawyer and has worked as a foreign service officer. One of his most widely read books is *Persona Non Grata*, which relates his experiences in Cuba, including his being kicked out of the island nation by dictator Fidel Castro. He continues to write and has become very involved in journalism and diplomacy.

Translated into many languages, José Donoso's books are about such subjects as the decadence of the elite, aging, sickness, and childhood demons. His novels and short stories are strikingly real and yet magical; *Curfew* and *The Garden Next Door* deal with politically charged topics such as exile. Donoso died in 1996 in Santiago at the age of 71.

Isabel Allende, a distant relative of President Salvador Allende, left Chile to live in Venezuela after Pinochet's takeover. There, she wrote her first novel, *La Casa de los Espíritus* (*House of the Spirits*), which tells the story of an aristocratic Chilean family ruled by a violent, autocratic, and passionate patriarch, Estéban, and his tender, clairvoyant wife, Clara. Based loosely on Allende's own childhood experiences, the novel is characteristic of the

Besides being a novelist, Jorge Edwards Valdés is also a lawyer, journalist, and diplomat.

"In Latin America, we value dreams, passions, obsessions, emotions, and all that which is very important to our lives has a place in literature—our sense of family, our sense of religion, our superstition, too."
—Isabel Allende, in an interview in 1985

Chilean children now have access to international movies and books and cartoon characters, although there are a few beloved Chilean originals. Condorito, a comic book character, is perhaps one of Chile's most successful exports. Condorito is a condor (a scavenger bird that thrives in the Andes) who has come to live in the human world. Mampato is a boy with a time travel belt who visits other places and other eras with his caveman sidekick, Ogú. Their adventures are both entertaining and educational. Papelucho is a little boy, created by author Marcela Paz in the 1960s, who survives the normal events and obstacles of life.

20th-century Latin American novel, filled with vivid, fantastical stories that place magical characters against a backdrop of a politically volatile and violent society.

Isabel Allende's subsequent novels, such as *Of Love and Shadows*, *Eva Luna*, *Paula*, *The Infinite Plan*, *Daughter of Fortune*, *My Invented Country*, *Portrait in Sepia*, and *Inés of My Soul* have been greeted with critical acclaim worldwide. She has made California her home for many years.

Ariel Dorfman is best known for his play *Death and the Maiden*, which is the story of a torture victim confronting her torturer. Exiled by the repressive Pinochet government, many of his works deal with human rights.

Antonio Skarmeta is a poet and novelist whose book *The Postman* was made into a popular movie. The DVD in the United States is called *Il Postino*. It spins a fictional tale of Pablo Neruda helping his love-struck mailman. His most recent novel, *Los Días del Arco Iris*, won a prestigious Latin American literary award in 2010.

While several of these established authors are still publishing well-received works, following the return to democracy, a new crop of acclaimed writers has emerged, including Jaime Collyer, Alberto Fuguet, Diamela Eltit, and Roberto Bolaño, who died in 2003.

Isabel Allende, author of numerous best-selling novels, has influenced Latin American literature.

MUSIC

An internationally important Chilean classical musician is pianist Claudio Arrau, who was one of the finest interpreters of the works of Beethoven. Chilean composers Enrique Soro and Juan Orrego are well known throughout Latin American.

The Nueva Canción, or New Song movement began in Chile in the early 1960s and spread to all of Latin America. Led by musician, visual artist, and poet Violeta Parra, the movement embraced issues of social protest and labor reform. It was filled with the revolutionary spirit of the time. Another prominent member of the movement was folk singer Victor Jara. He was arrested at the time of the military coup and was detained at the Chile Stadium, thereupon he sang protest songs! When he was killed by Chilean

Chileans light candles and play songs remembering Victor Jara, who was tortured and shot at the National Stadium in the 1973 Pinochet coup. Even to his death, he fought for the revolution, singing songs exalting love, peace, and social justice to raise insurgents' morale.

MUSIC FESTIVALS

Chile hosts one of the most important musical festivals in all of Latin America. The Festival de la Canción de Viña del Mar is held in this seaside resort every February. People from all over flock to Viña del Mar to attend this weeklong celebration of music. It is a competition with contestants from many different countries vying for the top prize. The festival is best known for the top-billed Latin American and North American artists who headline every evening's performance. Pop, hip-hop, reggaeton, and rock groups bring the audiences to their feet night after night. Artists who delight the audience most are awarded the Gaviota (Seagull) Trophy, and are begged by the fans to perform countless encores.

The Semanas Musicales de Frutillar is a classical music festival held in the beautiful lakeside town of Frutillar in the Lake District. There are also folk music festivals—Festival de la Patagonia, held in Punta Arenas, and Festival del Huaso, held in Olmué in central Chile. In 2011 Santiago hosted the Lollapalooza alternative rock music festival (right).

security forces, he became a martyr to many Chileans. The Chile Stadium has since been renamed Victor Jara Stadium in his honor.

Since that time, Chilean musicians have made their marks in the genres of rock, pop, jazz, reggaeton, and hip-hop. A number of Chilean groups have gained fans all across Latin America, such as La Ley, Los Jaivas, Los Tres, Illapu, Chico Trujillo, Denisse Malebrán, Francisca Valenzuela, and Ana Tijoux. Chileans also embrace English language songs, and on most radio stations you will hear a mix of Spanish and English hits. A new cadre of young folk musicians is appearing on the local music scene as well, reviving folkloric musical traditions.

FOLK ART

Browsers at local fairs will come upon crafts that are very specific to Chile and the Chilean experience. Many of the finest examples of craftwork are related to the lifestyle of the *huaso*, or Chilean cowboy. There are beautiful handwoven ponchos in rich red and blue tones, straw hats, delicately carved wooden stirrups, leather goods, and tiny figures made from horsehair, called *rari*. Lapis lazuli, a radiant, intensely blue stone, is used to make jewelry, figurines, boxes, chess sets, and other fine articles.

Young locals dancing the classic *cueca* at a festival.

INDIGENOUS CRAFTS The Mapuche people of Chile are well known for their textiles, pottery, and musical instruments, but they are perhaps most famous for their silver jewelry. Mapuche pieces display a very distinctive style—most notable are the large stickpins (for fastening shawls), head ornaments, and massive necklaces.

Replicas of Diaguita pottery are sold in handicraft stores in northern Chile and Santiago. Decorated with heads of llamas, birds, or black-and-white geometric designs over terra-cotta, Diaguita dishes and jugs display an elegant simplicity.

Pomaire, a town about 35 miles (56 km) southwest of Santiago, is known for its hand-molded pottery made from a dark clay scraped from the nearby mountains. The pieces of pottery are fired in large, old-fashioned kilns and then sold from traditional adobe houses nearby.

CUECA Most festivals and celebrations in Chile include the national folk dance, *cueca* (KWAY-kah), for which there are varying regional styles. Inspired by the ritual of a rooster stalking a hen, it is a dance of courtship. A man dressed as a *huaso* and a woman in a full skirt, each holding a handkerchief, dance subtly and expressively around each other as musicians play the guitar, tambourine, harp, and accordion while the audience claps, shouts, and stamps its feet to encourage the couple.

INTERNET LINKS

http://nobelprize.org/nobel_prizes/literature/laureates/1971/ neruda.html

The official website of the Nobel Prize Organizations provides biographies of its past winners. This page features Pablo Neruda, who won the Nobel Prize for poetry in 1971. There is a bibliography of his works, his acceptance speech, and other information. There is also a biography and bibliography for poet Gabriela Mistral, who won a Nobel Prize in 1945.

http://worldmusic.nationalgeographic.com/view/page.basic/ country/content.country/chile_56

The National Geographic Music website has information on Chilean musicians, including the martyred folk singer Victor Jara, Angel Parra, and Carlos Maza, as well as indigenous music. If you search for "nueva cancion" you will find information on the New Song Movement. Selected pieces can be listened to.

www.theartstory.org/artist-matta-roberto.htm

This website provides a detailed biography of Roberto Matta, Chile's most famous modern artist. Many of his surrealist paintings are on view here.

www.isabelallende.com/

This is internationally famed author Isabel Allende's official website. Found here is her biography and information on her many books. Past interviews, speeches, and publicity photos can be searched.

LEISURE

Enlarged chess and checkers sets provide mental and physical exercise for Chileans in the Plaza de Armas Osorno.

CHILEANS SPEND A LOT of time with their families. On Sundays, many family members gather to cook and share a large meal together. All important celebrations are observed with extended family, such as birthdays, Easter, Christmas, and other holidays.

Families with small children spend sunny afternoons in parks, even in winter. The children ride bikes, play soccer, or just run around and play on jungle gym equipment.

In wealthy families weekends may be spent swimming or playing golf or tennis. Many belong to country clubs and sports unions. When in Santiago, they may eat at an upscale restaurant and attend a concert or play. In the winter some wealthy Chileans take ski vacations at fine resorts just an hour or two from Santiago. In the summer they often vacation at sea resorts along Chile's coast, where many of them own a second home.

Sunbathers on the white sandy beach at Bahia Inglesa (English Bay) in north Chile.

11

Skiers enjoying the gentle, snowy slopes of Chile.

Middle-class families also take beach vacations, and they enjoy camping in the parks and campgrounds of the Andes and the Lake District. Santiaguinos (sahn-tee-ah-GEE-nohs), or residents of Santiago, may spend an evening out dining at one of the city's many good restaurants and then going to a movie.

On weekends, teenagers congregate at the shopping malls, just as teenagers do in the United States. In Santiago there are many multilevel shopping centers filled with shops that sell everything from French perfume to Japanese computer games. Teens and young adults from all sectors of society attend parties, many of which start very late, often after 10 P.M. During the day and early evening it is not unusual to see young couples walking hand in hand through Santiago's public parks.

SPORTS

Chileans are active participants in many of the same amateur sports that interest North Americans and Europeans. Chileans play tennis, volleyball, and basketball, and enjoy horseback riding, jogging, snow skiing, fishing, scuba diving, surfing, kayaking, and windsurfing.

SOCCER As in the rest of Latin America, the favorite sport in Chile is soccer, or *fútbol* (PHOOT-ball). Chile hosts major international matches that attract some 60,000 people to Santiago's Estadio Nacional (National Stadium). Chile's finest professional soccer players are likened to national heroes and are instantly recognized by nearly every Chilean.

In the countryside and the city alike, boys play soccer wherever they can: in the schoolyard, on the streets, in parks, and even at home. A shirt from a favorite team is a prized possession.

Matches between schools or soccer clubs are very competitive. The fiercest rivalry is between the country's two best teams, the Universidad de Chile team and the Colo-Colo team, named after a Mapuche chief. Chile was exuberantly proud of its 2010 national team that advanced to the second round of the World Cup.

SNOW SKIING The Andean mountain range close to Santiago and in the far southern provinces provides Chileans with ideal skiing country. The ski season (June to September) attracts thousands of international tourists to Chile's 14 ski centers.

Portillo is a world-famous ski resort about 100 miles (161 km) north of Santiago. The site of the 1966 World Championships, Portillo is said to have the finest competitive runs. Farellones, La Parva, and El Colorado, 30 miles (48 km) from Santiago, are in another popular resort area; some wealthy Santiaguinos own apartments in the Farellones area and spend weekends there. Other popular ski resorts can be found near Pucón, in the Lake District, where aficionados can ski on the Villarrica volcano. Resorts farther south,

Many Chileans belong to sports clubs, which were founded by various ethnic groups and retain those original connections. For example, Santiago is home to a German club, a British club, a Palestinian club, a French club, a Spanish club, an Israeli club, a Croatian club, and an Italian club.

Scouting boys setting out on a trek in the Altos del Lircay National Reserve.

near Punta Arenas, are the only places in all of South America where skiers can see the ocean as they descend the slopes. Another ski center, Termas de Chillán, has the longest chairlift in South America, some of the best open-slope skiing in the Andes, and natural hot springs for after-ski bathing.

Valle Nevado, the newest and most lavish ski resort in Chile, is about 40 miles (64 km) northeast of Santiago. For the confident weekender, it even has facilities for heli-skiing, a combination of skiing and hang gliding.

WATER SPORTS Chileans love the beach, and many flock to Viña del Mar and the nearby seaside communities each year to swim, tan, gamble at the casinos, stroll in the famous gardens, and eat fresh seafood in one of the restaurants overlooking the ocean. During the peak summer season the streets are filled with people shopping, searching out cafés, and riding in horse-drawn carriages called victorias.

Certain areas along the coast are famous for their waves and wind, such as Pichidangui and Pichilemu. Avid surfers and windsurfers descend upon these towns in the summer and sometimes even into the winter months.

Deep-sea and lake fishing are also popular sports in Chile. In the north people fish for tuna, bonito, swordfish, shark, and marlin; in the south fishing for trout is very common. Some of the best fishing in South America is found in the Lake District, about 320 miles (515 km) south of Santiago. Fly-fishing is the preferred activity in top-notch Chilean Patagonia lodges. Scuba diving, boating, and water-skiing are popular in many areas off the coast.

KITE FLYING In the 18th century, Catholic monks brought the first kites to Chile, and kite flying became an amusement for the upper classes. Today, Santiaguinos from all walks of life fly kites for fun and as sport from September, the beginning of spring, until the weather turns cold again. Kites are sold for about a dollar at small stalls set up on Santiago's street corners.

Thousands of Santiaguinos turn out each weekend to fly their kites in public parks, and the sky gets so dense with the soaring kites that it is difficult to tell one's own from another's. Many kite strings become intertwined, crossing and cutting one another, and a few kites may crash into trees and power lines.

Serious kite fliers belong to clubs like the Chilean Kite Fliers Association, which is divided into teams. In one type of competition, two five-member teams battle to snap the strings of all the opponents' kites. Kites dart across the sky, twirling, jumping, and diving to avoid their rivals' entries. The string must be of white cotton. Some may be sharpened with glass powder, which is illegal and has been known to cause serious injuries. Kite fliers often tape their fingers to avoid getting cut by the glass powder. Sometimes two men handle one kite: one controls movement, while the other releases string from the 1,000-yard (914-m) spool.

Cowboys chasing a cow at the rodeo. Chilean rodeo is a popular spectator sport because of its colorful costumes and the fine horsemanship displayed by the competing riders.

THE RODEO

Chilean rodeo, which has little in common with North American rodeo, has its roots in 16th-century colonial society and is still a much-loved leisure activity. The rodeo began when Spanish ranchers hosted annual cattle roundups in Santiago to show off their cattle-leading skills. Over time, the sport developed into a contest of skill and horsemanship with very specific rules. Today, the rodeo is the most popular sport after soccer.

Originally, teams of riders that competed in the rodeo were made up of landowners and their employees. Now the competing teams are comprised of partners or friends, usually members of the upper and middle classes, who

The Chilean movie industry resurfaced with the return of democracy. The prominent themes have slowly moved away from political issues, venturing into comedy, drama, social issues, and documentaries. Chilean movies are frequent entrants at international film festivals, and some have achieved widespread critical praise. La Nana (The Maid), directed by Sebastian Silva, is a recent example. Director Andres Wood has made several highly acclaimed movies that depict the Chilean experience.

Television in Chile was introduced in the early 1960s, developed first by the universities and later by the state. It became a highly political medium in the 1970s and was subject to strict controls during the military government. Today broadcast television is a competitive media with a wide range of programming that includes children's shows, news programs, sitcoms, dramas (called telenovelas), and reality shows. Cable television, moreover, provides access to international programming from a number of countries in Latin America, North America, and Europe.

own farms and horses. Rodeo teams often travel from village to village with their families and stay in one another's homes. The teams are called *colleras* (koh-YEH-ras), and the horses receive as much recognition as the riders.

Also known as *la fiesta huasa* (lah fee-ESS-tah WAH-sah), the rodeo takes place in many towns throughout central and southern Chile in arenas called *media lunas* (MEH-dee-ah LOO-nahs), or half moons.

The competition begins when pairs of *huasos* enter the ring in pursuit of a young bull. The riders wear traditional *huaso* gear—flat-topped hats, colorful short-cropped ponchos, fringed leggings, and pointed boots with spurs—and equip their horses with festive saddles.

In the rodeo ring the riders take up positions at the flank and rear of the bull. Their aim is to force the bull to stop at a certain place on the wall, without using a lasso. Judges award points according to where the horse touches the bull: no points are given for a block on the neck, but two points are given for the shoulder blade, three for behind the shoulder blade, and four for the back legs, the most difficult part for the horse to make a block on. The riders try three times on each of three bulls, changing their positions each time.

Chile won its first Olympic gold medal in 2004 when Nicolás Massú and Fernando González won the finals match in men's doubles tennis.

Although Chilean rodeo might sound a bit tame to fans of North American bronco-busting, it is quite entertaining to Chileans, who appreciate fine horsemanship. The bulls are not harmed, although some animal rights activists object to the contest. Riders occasionally do have a brush with danger, such as when they collide with a frightened 800-pound (363-kg) bull.

Before the rodeo it is customary to gather in a large shed outside the *media luna* to eat empanadas and drink good Chilean wine. After the event the crowd cheers the winning riders, who receive trophies or certificates—no money—as prizes. After the prize ceremony the crowd gathers around as the leading *huaso* dances the *cueca* with the rodeo queen and sings a *tonada* (toh-NAH-dah)—a touching, sentimental song that is the equivalent of a North American country ballad—about a lost love, sadness, or an emotional upset.

Rodeos are a treasured symbol of national pride, and many are held around Chile's Independence Day, in September.

INTERNET LINKS

www.chile.travel

This website is the official travel guide to Chile, administered by SERNATUR, the National Service for Tourism. It provides information on what to do, where to go, and special events in Chile. It covers topics such as sports, nature, culture, relaxation, and astronomy.

www.gochile.cl/en

GoChile's website provides information on many leisure activities, such as skiing, fly fishing, mountain biking, hot springs immersion, rafting, horseback riding, paragliding, and more. It provides information on the history of these activities and their current status.

www.santiagotourist.com

This website details 30 sights and activities you must see and do when visiting Santiago.

Chile is fast becoming a destination for adventure tourism. The south has many travel operators offering white-water rafting, kayaking, zip lining (aerial rope sliding), rock climbing, hiking, biking and many other experiences.

FESTIVALS

A Chilean dressed in a flamboyant costume and mask for a festival in Antofagasta.

12

THE MOST COLORFUL FESTIVALS in Chile are religious in origin, such as La Tirana and Domingo de Cuasimodo, although the biggest celebration of the year is September 18, Chile's Independence Day.

Patron saints' days are celebrated with small processions in which villagers carry images of their town's particular saint through the streets. On June 29, the feast of Saint Peter, the image of the patron saint of fishermen, is taken out in a decorated boat to the breakwater to bless the first catch of the day. Very often there are groups on hand dancing in devotion to Saint Peter. It is believed that by so doing, they will be blessed with bountiful fish harvests. Saint Peter celebrations are

Chileans look forward all year to September 18, a fervent celebration of the nation's independence, when the entire population erupts with national pride.

Folkloric dancers bring a flurry of colors to a festival in Chile.

January 1	New Year's Day
March/April	Good Friday/Holy Saturday/Easter
May 1	Labor Day
May 21	Navy Day
May/June	Corpus Christi
June 29	Feast of Saints Peter and Paul (holiday on nearest Monday)
August 15	Assumption of the Virgin Mary
September 18	Independence Day
September 19	Army Day
October 12	Columbus Day (holiday on nearest Monday)
November 1	All Saints' Day
December 8	Immaculate Conception
December 25	Christmas Day

held in cities and little villages and coves all along the Pacific coast. On the Feast of Our Lady of Mount Carmel, schoolchildren, government officials, members of sports clubs, and other devotees pay homage to the patroness of Chile.

Celebrations honoring Saint Isidore (patron saint of peasants in northern Chile), the Lady of Lo Vazquez, and Saint Sebastian are especially popular. Besides providing community solidarity, holidays and festivals in Chile are cherished family occasions.

EASTER IN THE COUNTRYSIDE

A religious tradition unique to Chile is held in villages throughout central Chile on the Sunday after Easter. Called Domingo de Cuasimodo (taken from a Latin phrase used during the Easter Mass that refers to Christ's resurrection), the festival is celebrated with great fanfare. Houses are decorated, and members of the traditional procession wear costumes and parade through the village

New Year's Eve is prominently a family-centered celebration in Chile, primarily because it takes place in the middle of the summer. People celebrate with barbeques and family gatherings. Fireworks erupt in the sky at midnight, and Chileans embrace as they wish each other a happy new year. (It is considered unlucky to wish someone a happy new year before the stroke of midnight.) In Santiago the fireworks are set off around the tall communications tower downtown and from other high buildings toward the mountains. The most famous fireworks displays are along the coast, however, with Valparaíso's being the most spectacular and best known. Once the fireworks are over, Chileans begin to make their rounds, visiting family and friends until the wee small hours of the morning. There are several superstitions surrounding the new year. Many Chileans will eat a spoonful of lentils for good luck. Others will put money and bus or plane tickets in their pockets to ensure wealth and travel in the year ahead.

on horseback, holding pennants and images of Christ. Families save up for a year to decorate the carriages and floats they ride in during the pageant. Horsemen don their finest *huaso* attire and drape their mounts in splendid capes that resemble those worn by the horses of knights in the Middle Ages.

The festival has a fascinating history. In the 19th century, after independence, groups of bandits terrorized rural communities outside Chile's larger cities. Outlaws like the Pincheira brothers, who dominated the territory south of Santiago, scared away even government troops. They stole valuables from farmers and sacred objects such as gold cups and costly vestments from priests traveling to their outlying parishes.

To protect the priests, armed *huasos* began to escort them on their travels. Dressed in brightly colored riding outfits, the *huasos* would storm through the countryside ahead of the procession, holding an image of Christ and daring the thieves to challenge them.

Townspeople in the mood of Domingo de Cuasimodo in Chile.

Looking smart! A military formation at the Independence Day parade.

After the bandit attacks had been stopped, the festivity became a religious tradition as well as a chance to show off one's finest *huaso* garb. Today, ranchers and farmers participate in the Cuasimodo dressed in colorful cloaks and black trousers. Instead of wearing the traditional flat hat, they tie white handkerchiefs around their heads as a sign of respect. Their dress is Spanish in origin, but their fast riding style, as they gallop alongside the priests' carriages, is reminiscent of the Mapuche, who became expert horsemen in their battles against the Spaniards.

Riders escort priests, who ride in decorated coaches. As they parade through the villages, the elderly and the sick come to the doors and windows of their houses to receive Holy Communion. Men, women, and children follow the lead coach in horse-drawn carriages, floats, or—in towns where horses are not as readily available—on bicycles or motorcycles.

CHILEAN INDEPENDENCE DAY

Independence Day is a grand affair in Chile. This day provides Chileans the opportunity to demonstrate their patriotism. Throughout the month of September, Chilean flags are flown in front of houses and mounted on cars.

On September 18, Chileans spend the day eating empanadas and drinking red wine and *chicha* (CHEE-chah), a fermented grape drink. Many people attend *fondas* (FOHN-dahs), or fairs, that offer lots of food and drink, music and dancing, rodeos, arts and crafts, and sometimes shows, complete with dancing groups and horseback riding.

People gather to dance the *cueca* in public squares and in private homes. Two types of outfits are worn. In the simple version, men dress as *huasos* and women wear full calico skirts. In the more elegant version, men don a more refined *huaso* costume and women wear white ruffled blouses under

Every division of the Chilean Armed Forces is represented in the Independence Day parade. One of the most interesting is the Special Mountain Troops Group, dressed in white with skis strapped to their backs, accompanied by Saint Bernard dogs.

Navy Day, celebrated on May 21, honors the heroism of Agustín Arturo Prat Chacón, the navy's foremost hero, who fought in the naval battle of Iquique in 1879 during the War of the Pacific. Captain Prat, outnumbered and certain to be defeated by Peruvian forces, refused to surrender his ship, La Esmeralda. He and his crew members fearlessly boarded the enemy vessel and perished during the battle. News of his bravery galvanized the Chilean people and Chile eventually won the war.

cropped black jackets with a long narrow black skirt. The *cueca* symbolizes the classical ritual of courtship. Lively crowds clap and cheer the dancers on.

The next day, September 19, is Army Day. The armed forces stage a large parade in Santiago, attended by the president and other government officials. Most people watch the parade, which lasts for several hours, on television. Smaller parades are held in towns and villages throughout the country.

THE FESTIVAL OF LA TIRANA

Some 150,000 people gather in the village of La Tirana near the Atacama Desert to offer devotion to the Virgin Mary each July. Many are members of dance and music clubs called *chinos* (CHEE-nohs) that come to honor the Virgin or to give thanks for favors she has granted during the year.

The musicians play trumpets, trombones, cymbals, and drums amid a group of dancers, who dance for three days straight, pausing only to eat and change their costumes. The dancers say that they need neither stimulants nor alcohol to keep going, because their faith spurs them on. After the dances, the performers make a pilgrimage to the Church of la Virgen del Carmen.

The village of La Tirana, which means "The Tyrant," got its name from an Indian princess who, after being converted to Catholicism, became a tyrant in her efforts to convert the rest of her people. Her people murdered her for her disloyalty, but a priest later succeeded in converting them all. A sanctuary was built to honor the princess and the Virgin Mary. Devout Catholics have come here to pray ever since.

TAPATI FESTIVAL

Every summer the inhabitants of Easter Island, or Rapa Nui, celebrate the Tapati Festival. Participants honor their Rapa Nui culture with indigenous dances, chants, and song. There are also various competitions in woodcarving, spearfishing, horse racing, and *kai kai*. This is a dexterity game whereby figures are created out of string via finger movements. Subsequent movements alter the figure. The player, meanwhile, sings a song describing how the original settlers on the island had built boats and sailed across the ocean to Rapa Nui, then dismantled the boats to build their first homes.

CHRISTMAS IN CHILE

There are two major differences between Christmas in Chile and Christmas in North America. In Chile, Christmas arrives in the middle of summer and is, therefore, not associated with snow, but with barbecues. Also, although large department stores decorate their windows, and Christmas trees, presents, and Santa Claus (called *el viejito pascuero*, or little old man of Christmas) are very common, there is still an emphasis on the birth of Christ.

Christmas decorations at the University of La Serena in Coquimbo. Unlike Christmas in North America, Christmas in Chile comes in summer.

In mid-December, many Catholic families set up nativity scenes at home. Some are very simple, with only small images of Joseph, Mary, the Christ Child, and perhaps a cow; others are elaborate, featuring the countryside, the Three Wise Men, angels, shepherds, and many animals. In upper-class families, the nativity figures may be made of the finest materials and are passed down through generations. In poorer families, whose nativity figures may be made from clay or cardboard, the figure of Christ is often made of porcelain. There are even nativity scenes that occupy whole rooms and include such props as grass, roads, hills, and tiny villagers.

On Christmas Eve, Chileans attend a midnight Mass called *misa de gallo* (MEE-sah deh GAH-yoh), or Rooster's Mass, and sit down to a sumptuous holiday supper afterward. They also open their gifts at that time. Christmas Day is often a quiet family day, when relatives visit and exchange presents. Traditional cakes and drinks are served.

An alcoholic drink called *cola de mono* (KOH-lah day MOH-noh), or "monkey's tail," is made during the Christmas season. It contains a powerful alcohol called *aguardiente* (ah-gwahr-dee-EHN-teh), coffee, milk, sugar, cinnamon, and egg yolk. A rich spice cake or bread full of candied fruits and nuts, called *pan de pascua* (pahn day PAHS-kwah), or "Christmas bread," is also a Chilean Christmas treat.

INTERNET LINKS

http://spotlightchile.com/cueca.htm

This website explains the history of the *cueca*, Chile's national dance, which is a main component of Independence Day celebrations every September 18. The page also includes a photo of a *cueca* performance and sketches outlining the dance's choreography.

www.allaboutchiletravel.com/chile-easter-island-festival.htm

This online travel guide provides fascinating information on the Tapati Festival held every summer on Easter Island (Rapa Nui). It details the history of the festival and its main components, the sporting activities, and ritual dances.

www.letsgochile.com/locations/big-north/tarapacai/la-tirana

This travel site offers the history behind the festival of la Virgen de La Tirana held every July in the northern town of La Tirana. There are also photographs of the festival, with its brightly colored devil costumes.

Tijerales (tee-herr-AH-lays) is the Spanish word for the roof support structure of a building. Once this phase of construction has been completed, a Chilean flag is raised on the roof of the building, construction is halted, and a barbecue is held for the workers to celebrate the fact that the final stage of construction has been reached.

FOOD

Fresh fruits and vegetables being sold at the Mercado Central (the Central Market) of Santiago.

13

A PROFUSION OF DELICIOUS foods are piled high in Chilean markets. Such fresh fruits as strawberries, raspberries, grapes, melons, bananas, figs, pears, avocados, apricots, and peaches are plentiful. Corn, squash, potatoes, eggplant, and other fresh vegetables including garlic, carrots, peppers, tomatoes, and beans, also exist in large quantities.

But most impressive of all local fare are the seafood stalls, overflowing with a bounty of fish and shellfish straight from nearby waters.

Chileans enjoy seafood. The icy cold Humboldt Current, which flows north from Antarctica into the Pacific waters off Chile, provides the country with some of the world's finest and most unusual fish. *Locos* (LOH-kohs), which are similar to abalone; *machas* (MAH-chahs), or razor clams; *erizos* (eh-REE-sos), sea urchins the size of tennis balls; *camarones* (kah-mah-ROH-nehs), or shrimp; langostinos (lahng-gohs-TEE-nohs), tiny rock lobsters; and *congrio* (KON-gree-oh), or conger eel, are Chilean favorites.

Chilean cuisine developed from both indigenous and European influences. For example, *porotos granados* (poh-ROH-tos grah-NAH-dos), a bean stew, combines the indigenous ingredients of corn, squash, and beans and distinctly Spanish ingredients such as onions and garlic. Another popular dish with indigenous origins is *humitas* (ooh-MEE-tahs). This is ground corn mixed with milk, basil, and onions. The mixture is wrapped in corn husks and boiled. Meals are usually accompanied by Chilean wine.

Among middle-
and upper-class
families, the lady
of the house does
not spend much
time in the kitchen,
because there will
probably be a maid
to do the cooking
and cleaning. With
the increase in
Peruvian household
help, ethnic
Peruvian cuisine has
been introduced into
the Chilean home.

CHILEAN SPECIALTIES

POROTOS GRANADOS Loved by all Chileans, this quintessential national dish is made of corn, beans, squash, onions, and garlic. The main ingredient of this vegetarian stew, cranberry beans, is grown almost year-round in the central region, which has a mild, stable climate. If fresh cranberry beans are not available, dried cranberry or navy beans are a good substitute. Some Chileans like to eat the stew topped with a spoonful of *pebre* (PEH-breh), a hot sauce of onions, vinegar, olive oil, garlic, coriander, and chili.

EMPANADAS These pastries are stuffed with meat, cheese, or seafood. *Empanadas de pino* are filled with meat, onions, raisins, a black olive, and a hard-cooked egg. The turnovers are baked until the crust is lightly browned. Chileans eat empanadas as a snack or as the first course of the main meal, often with red wine. Heaps of hot empanadas are served at festivals and celebrations and at rodeos.

PASTEL DE CHOCLO Most often served in pottery from Pomaire, this typical Chilean summer dish consists of a large piece of chicken and a ground meat mixture similar to that found in empanadas, covered by ground corn, and baked in the oven. Chileans sprinkle sugar on top before eating.

CURANTO This specialty comes from Chiloé, in southern Chile. The dish consists of shellfish, meat, potatoes, *milcaos* (potato pancakes), *chapaleles* (potato and wheat dumplings), and various types of bread. The food is wrapped in big leaves and placed over red-hot rocks in a hole in the ground. It is then covered with dirt so that it slowly cooks for a number of hours.

CONGRIO Conger eel is a gourmet treat in Chile. It is not an eel, but a long, nearly boneless, firm-fleshed fish with a small tail. It can be baked, grilled, fried, or stewed. The fish comes in three varieties: black, gold, and red (the rarest and tastiest). *Caldillo de congrio* (kahl-DEE-yoh deh KON-/gree-oh), a soup of conger eel, tomatoes, potatoes, onions, herbs, and spices, is a national delicacy. It is traditionally stewed in an earthen pot to seal in the seasoning and give it its hearty flavor.

ALCOHOLIC BEVERAGES

Chileans, like the French and Italians, are avid wine drinkers. They may have wine at lunch and dinner, or at the cocktail hour, and at home and in restaurants.

Chilean wines are of high quality and are reasonably priced. They are a source of national pride. Wine critics liken Chilean wines to French rather than Californian wines in flavor. The best vineyards are found in the Central Valley, which has what is known as a Mediterranean climate—warm summer, dry fall, and mild spring.

The Chilean wine industry made an exciting discovery in 1994. The Carmenère grape was thought to be extinct, having fallen victim to a blight in Europe in the mid-19th century. The grape had actually been transplanted to Chile and survived, but was thought for many years to be a Merlot grape. Since the felicitous discovery, Chile has produced and marketed Carmenère.

An extremely popular alcoholic drink in Chile, *pisco* (PEES-koh), is also made from grapes. Almost colorless, with a light bouquet, *pisco* does not taste strong, but it is. It can be served by itself, mixed with ginger ale, cola, or vermouth, or in its most preferred form, as the main ingredient in a *pisco* sour—a frothy cocktail made with *pisco*, lemon juice, sugar, ice, and beaten egg white.

Chicha, a fermented grape-juice drink that tastes similar to apple cider, and *aguardiente*, or "fire water," a potent brandy distilled from grapes, are often served at holidays. *Chicha* is drunk at Independence Day celebrations.

At Christmastime, Chileans celebrate with *Cola de Mono* (monkey's tail). This drink mixes *pisco* with coffee, milk, eggs, sugar, vanilla, and spices.

Curanto is a rich southern dish traditionally cooked in a pit dug into the ground and covered with hot rocks. Ingredients include beef, pork, chicken, lamb, potatoes, peas, beans, lobsters, mussels, oysters, and clams.

OTHER BEVERAGES

Chile is not a coffee-drinking nation. A diner who orders a *café* will get a cup of hot water and a small jar of instant coffee; coffee made from freshly

Food   **125**

ground beans is costly. Chileans order *café café* to get good brewed coffee or espresso, often at a coffee bar. A *café con leche* (kah-FAY kon LEH-chay), coffee with milk, is one spoonful of coffee in a cup of hot milk. With the arrival of Starbucks, however, a new variety of coffee drinker is being developed.

Most Chileans prefer traditional tea to coffee, a long-lasting legacy of the British immigrants. Chileans enjoy tea not only at afternoon tea (*once*), but also after lunch and dinner. Some people may drink herbal teas such as camomile, called *aguitas* (agh-WEE-tahs), to help with digestion. A popular herbal infusion called yerba maté is made from the leaves of a shrub belonging to the holly berry family. Enjoyed primarily by rural people in the south, yerba maté is made by mixing the ground, greenish herb with hot water and drinking it through a *bombilla* (bom-BEE-yah), a metal straw with a bulb-shaped filter at the base. The tea container is passed around and everybody drinks from the same straw. Some *bombillas* are beautifully decorated or even made of silver. The tea is taken in small quantities in view of its high caffeine content.

Children and adults alike have a sweet tooth, as evidenced by the amount of sugar mixed into their tea and coffee. Chileans tend to drink a lot of soda and juices—even those freshly made in restaurants have a lot of added sugar.

EATING OUT IN CHILE

Although Chileans prefer eating at home, they do have an inviting variety of restaurants to choose from, at least in the larger cities. Santiago, Valparaíso, and Concepción have everything from fine dining establishments to hamburger counters and typical Chilean restaurants in between. Many restaurants serve traditional Chilean specialties and seafood. Others offer Chinese, French, and Spanish menus. Cuisine from neighboring Latin American countries is easily found, and there are growing numbers of exotic restaurants, such as Indian, Mexican, and Middle Eastern.

Bars in Chile serve light snacks and drinks. Most pubs sell only alcoholic beverages, although some serve empanadas and light sandwiches. *Fuentes de soda* (foo-EHN-tehs deh SOH-dah), or soda fountains, serve soft drinks, fruit juices, and beer. *Parilladas* (pah-ree-YAH-dahs) offer steaks and other food cooked on charcoal grills. *Confiterías* (kohn-fee-teh-REE-ahs) are cake shops that also serve coffee and tea. *Cafeterías* and *hosterías* (ohs-teh-REE-ahs) are simple eateries. Fast-food chains like McDonald's and the local Doggies have sprouted up all over Chile.

Many Chilean restaurants offer a set meal called a *menú-del-día* (meh-NEW-dell-DEE-ah) for lunch and dinner. This very economical meal often consists of a hearty soup, a main course of chicken or meat with a side dish and soft drink and dessert. Diners may have to pay extra if they want a salad or vegetables to accompany their meal. The waiter, called *garzón* (gar-SOHN), will expect an additional tip for good service.

All along the coast there are both simple and expensive restaurants that serve fresh seafood. A favorite order is the diner's choice of fish served with *salsa margarita*, a sauce that includes mussels, clams, and shrimp.

Vegetarians used to have a very hard time finding meals, but the number of vegetarian restaurants in cities has increased. The goodness of Chilean fresh produce inspires many fine dishes.

A popular sweet is fried dough sprinkled with powdered sugar called *calzones rotos* (cal-ZOHN-ays ROH-tohs), which translates as "torn underwear," because of the shape of the dough.

Dried clams and mussels hanging in a market stall in Puerto Montt.

MEALTIMES AND TYPICAL MEALS

Breakfast time in Chile is between 7 and 9 A.M. The average breakfast consists of toast and instant coffee or brewed tea—no grains. Some Chileans eat large breakfasts of ham and scrambled eggs. Lunch is typically served at about 1 or 1:30 P.M. and goes on until about 3 P.M. It is the largest meal of the day and often consists of a first course of soup or empanadas, a main course of seafood, chicken, or a meat stew, side dishes such as vegetables or potatoes, and ice cream and fruit for dessert.

Afternoon tea in Chile is called *once*. There are a number of stories on the origin of the name *once*. Some say that it comes from the British custom of having "elevenses"—a short tea break taken at around 11 A.M.—(*once* means "eleven"). Others attribute it to the miners who, though not allowed to consume alcohol in the mines, secretly added *aguardiente* to their tea; since there are 11 letters in *aguardiente*, it is said that miners began referring to their afternoon "tea" as *once*.

Like Europeans, Chileans dine very late. During the week, dinner is served between 8 and 9 P.M.; on weekends, after 9 P.M. Most restaurants do not open until 9 P.M. At dinner parties, the meal is often served as late as 10 P.M. Dinner food is similar to lunch food and is followed by coffee or herbal tea. Wine and beer are often served, too.

A family having a meal in a restaurant in Chile.

TABLE AND PARTY ETIQUETTE

Chileans follow certain rules at the table and in social gatherings. When expected at a dinner party, it is appropriate to arrive about 15 minutes late. If invited for cocktails, the guest will probably be asked to stay for dinner as well. The host and hostess will be given flowers or chocolates. At a formal gathering, it is considered rude to eat anything, even typical "finger food," using only the hands. At sit-down dinners, maids serve each guest a full plate of food. Buffets are also common. Good manners require one to eat a little of everything on the plate, even if some of the food is not to one's liking. When serving wine to someone seated nearby at a dinner party, the bottle must be held in the right hand.

Often, maids will clear away the dishes and clean up, so it is improper to offer to help. When the meal is over, it is important to spend time talking to and thanking the host and hostess before saying good-bye. Thank-you notes are not necessary in Chile, but a short telephone call is made the day after the party.

INTERNET LINKS

www.food.com/recipes/chilean

This popular recipe website offers many recipes for Chilean cuisine. It is divided into categories such as heirloom meals, holiday meals, and vegetarian meals.

www.southamerica.cl/Chile/Food.htm

Providing information on typical foods and snacks, this website also offers links to typical drinks and tips on the cuisine found in Chile.

www.foodbycountry.com/Algeria-to-France/Chile.html

This site intertwines history and information on Chilean food with some of the country's most popular recipes.

www.winesofchile.org

A promotional site put together by over 90 Chilean wineries, including all of the top-rated producers. Additionally, it provides information on wines, wine growing regions, and industry news.

PASTEL DE CHOCLO (CORN AND MEAT PIE)

This typical Chilean summer dish serves six.

Kernels from six ears of corn, grated

4 leaves of finely chopped fresh basil

½ teaspoon (2.5 ml) salt

1½ tablespoons (22.5 ml) butter

¼ to ½ (60—125 ml) cup milk

1 large onion, chopped

1½ tablespoons (22.5 ml) oil

½ pound (225 g) finely ground lean beef

Salt and pepper to taste

½ teaspoon (2.5 ml) ground cumin

2 hard-cooked eggs, sliced

Handful of olives

½ cup (125 ml) raisins

6 pieces of chicken, browned in hot oil,
    seasoned with salt, pepper, and ground cumin

1 tablespoon (15 ml) confectioners' sugar

Heat the corn kernels, chopped basil, salt, and butter in a large pot. Add milk slowly, stirring constantly until the mixture thickens. Cook over low heat for 5 minutes. Set aside. Fry the onions in oil until they are transparent. Add the ground meat and stir until brown. Season with salt, pepper, and ground cumin.

To prepare the pie, use an ovenproof dish that can be taken to the table. Spread the ground meat mixture over the bottom of the dish. Arrange the hard-cooked egg slices, olives, and raisins over the mixture. Put the chicken pieces on top; bone the chicken pieces first if preferred. Cover the filling with the set-aside corn mixture. Sprinkle the confectioners' sugar over the top. Bake in a hot oven at 400ºF (205ºC) for 30 to 35 minutes until the crust is golden brown. Serve at once.

CAZUELA DE AVE (CHILEAN CHICKEN SOUP)

This chicken soup serves six.

1 medium chicken, skinned and boned

1½ tablespoons (22.5 ml) oil

½ onion, sliced thinly

½ red bell pepper cut in ribbons

1 celery stalk, sliced

1 teaspoon (5 ml) ground oregano

4 cups (1 L) cold water

Salt and pepper to taste

4 potatoes cut in half

1 heaped tablespoon (15 ml) of uncooked rice

½ cup (125 ml) pumpkin seeds

Cut chicken into bite-size pieces. Add oil to a cooking pot and fry chicken over medium heat. Add onions and sauté. Add pepper, celery, oregano, salt, pepper, and water. Bring to a boil and simmer for about 15 minutes. Add potatoes and rice, turn down heat, cover with lid, and simmer for 20 minutes. Soften pumpkin seeds with a little bit of broth, then add the seeds to pot. Serve hot.

MAP OF CHILE

Aconcagua River, B2—B3

Andes mountain range, B1—B3, C1—C2

Antofagasta, B1

Argentina, B2—B5, C1—C5, D2—D3

Arica, B1

Atacama Desert, B1—B2

Atlantic Ocean, C3—C5, D2—D5

Bío-Bío River, B3

Bolivia, C1, D1

Brazil, D1—D3

Calama, C1

Cape Horn, C5

Chiloé Island, B4

Chonos Archipelago, B4

Concepción, B3

Copiapó, B2

Coquimbo, B2

Cordillera Occidental, B1, C1

Easter Island, A2

Hanga Roa, A2

Incahuasi Mt., C2

Iquique, B1

Itata River, B3

Juan Fernández Islands, B3

Lake District, B3—B4

La Serena, B2

Llullaillaco Mt., C2

Lota, B3

Magallanes, B5

Maipo River, B3

Maunga Terevaka Mt., A2

Maule River, B3

Mercedario Mt., B2

Ojos del Salado Mt., C2

Osorno, B4

Pacific Ocean, A1—A5, B1—B5

Paraguay, C1—C2, D1—D2

Patagonia, B4—B5

Peru, B1, C1

Puerto Montt, B4

Punta Arenas, B5

Rancagua, B3

San Antonio, B3

Santiago, B3

Strait of Magellan, B5, C5

Talca, B3

Talcahuano, B3

Temuco, B3

Tierra del Fuego, C5

Tropic of Capricorn, A1, B1, C1, D1

Tupungato Mt., B3

Uruguay, D2—D3

Valdivia, B3

Valparaíso, B3

Viña del Mar, B3

Volcán Rana Kao, A2

Volcán Rana Roraka, A2

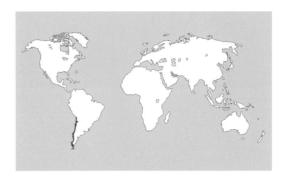

ECONOMIC CHILE

Natural Resources

 Animal products

 Fishing

 Forestry

 Mining

Agriculture

 Dairy products

 Fruit

 Grape brandy

 Wine

Services

 Duty free zone

 Financial center

 Port

 Tourism

ABOUT THE ECONOMY

OVERVIEW
Chile has a stable and robust economy. It enjoyed many years of strong economic growth from the 1990s up until the economic crisis of 2008. Much of this growth was due to exports such as fruit, wine, copper, wood products, and fish. While the country did not escape the worldwide financial crisis of 2008, it was not as severely affected as many other countries. Chile's fiscally responsible policies had provided the country with substantial monetary reserves that it could tap during the crisis. Even though employment and export levels had dropped, overall the country's economy is doing well and is nicely poised to take advantage of world economic recovery.

GROSS DOMESTIC PRODUCT (GDP)
$260 billion (2010 estimate)

GDP SECTORS
Agriculture 5.6 percent, industry and manufacturing 40.5 percent, and services 53.9 percent (2009 estimate)

INFLATION RATE
1.7 percent (2010 estimate)

CURRENCY
1 Chilean peso (Ch$) = 100 centavos
$1 = 450 Ch$ (It normally fluctuates between 450 and 477 pesos to the dollar.) (May 2011 estimate)
Notes: 500, 1,000, 2,000, 5,000, 10,000, 20,000; Coins: 1, 5, 10, 50, 100

LAND AREA
292,136 square miles (756,630 square km)

WORKFORCE
7.58 million (2010 estimate): Agriculture and fishing 12 percent; mining 3 percent; manufacturing 11 percent; construction 8 percent; trade and services 50 percent (which can be broken down as follows— trade 21 percent, transportation 7 percent, utilities 1 percent, hotel and restaurant 4 percent, banking 2 percent, real estate 6 percent, domestic services 6 percent, and other services 3 percent); public sector 5 percent; health care 4 percent; education 6 percent; and other 1 percent

UNEMPLOYMENT RATE
8.5 percent (2011 estimate)

AGRICULTURAL PRODUCTS
Apples and other fruit, potatoes, onions, garlic, beans, tomatoes, beef, fish, poultry, sugar beets, timber, wheat, wine, wool, and dairy products.

MAJOR EXPORTS
Copper, cellulose, fish and fish meal, fresh fruit and vegetables, wine, pork, wood, and wood products

MAJOR IMPORTS
Chemicals, electronics, machinery, oil, tools, vehicles, and vehicle parts

MAIN TRADING PARTNERS
China, United States, Japan, Brazil, South Korea, Argentina, and Mexico

POVERTY RATE
11.5 percent (2009 estimate)

CULTURAL CHILE

La Tirana Festival
Annual festival held on July 16 in honor of the Virgin of Carmen. Dance groups called *Chinos* parade through the village of La Tirana in exotic costumes to ask the Virgin for favors or give thanks for favors granted.

Moais
Easter Island's stone carvings, mostly of male heads and torsos, are surrounded by mystery. The islanders call their island Rapa Nui.

Festival de la Canción
This annual music festival is a feast for pop music fans.

Pablo Neruda Museum
The museum celebrates the life and works of the Nobel Prize-winning writer.

Wine Route
Delightful route through Chile's beautiful wine-producing valleys.

University of Concepión quarter
One of Chile's oldest universities, it is named after the town where it is located.

German Colonization Museum
This outdoor museum exhibits the life and work of early German settlers.

Pintados
These hillside geoglyphs date from A.D. 1000–1400 and are national monuments.

María Elena and Pedro de Valdivia
Tours of the last functioning nitrate mines and their towns

San Pedro de Atacama/Valle de la Luna
Valle de la Luna, or Moon Valley, is a small valley of dried-up salt-covered lakes with a few small hills. It gives visitors the impression of being on the moon.

Ojos del Salado
World's highest active volcano at 22,615 feet (6,893 m)

Pre-Columbian Museum; National History Museum; Museum of Fine Arts
A variety of museums offer a wide range of visual treats.

Historic Museum of Coal
This museum showcases artifacts from early coal mining days.

Mapuche Museum
This museum showcases the culture and history of the Mapuche. It includes an authentic ruco dwelling.

Araucanía Regional Museum
The Temuco region is home to many Mapuche people. This museum showcases the culture and history of this indigenous people.

Valdivia History Museum
This museum features a collection of items from Spanish colonial days and from the early period of German immigration.

Chiloé Island
Known for its Palafitos, or houses built on stilts over the water with boats anchored underneath at low tide. Also known for distinct wooden churches built in the 18th and 19th centuries, many of which are national monuments.

Torres del Paine National Park
This park offers a spectacular hiking circuit.

ABOUT THE CULTURE

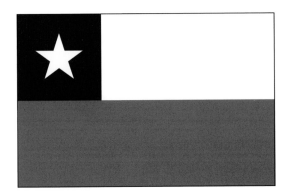

OFFICIAL NAME
Republic of Chile

CAPITAL
Santiago

OTHER MAJOR CITIES
Antofagasta, Arica, Concepción, Iquique, Puerto Montt, Temuco, Valparaíso, Viña del Mar, and Punta Arenas

FLAG
The design of the current Chilean flag was influenced by the U.S. and French flags. There are two equal horizontal bands of white (top) and red; a blue square the same height as the white band at the hoist-side end of the white band; the square bears a white five-pointed star (a Mapuche symbol) in the center, representing a guide to progress and honor; blue symbolizes the sky, white is for the snow-covered Andes, and red represents the blood spilled to achieve independence.

POPULATION
16,888,760 (2011 estimate)

LIFE EXPECTANCY
77.7 years (2011 estimate)

ETHNIC GROUPS
Primarily Spanish and Spanish mixed with indigenous groups such as the Mapuche, with some German, Croatian, English, French, Italian, and Middle Eastern (Palestinian). Recent immigration of Koreans, Peruvians, and other Latin Americans.

TIME
Chilean standard time (winter months: May to August) Greenwich mean time: 4 hours; Chilean daylight savings time (summer months: August to May) Greenwich mean time: 3 hours

RELIGIONS
Roman Catholic 70 percent; Evangelical 15.1 percent; Jehovah's Witness 1.1 percent; other Christian 1 percent; other, including Jewish, 4.6 percent; none 8.3 percent (2002 estimate)

NATIONAL FLOWER
Copihue, a red or pink bell-shaped flower from the lily family (also known as the Chilean bellflower and Chilean glory flower)

NATIONAL DANCE
Cueca. A man and a woman dance artfully back and forth and around each other in this mannered courtship dance, waving handkerchiefs above their heads.

OFFICIAL LANGUAGE
Spanish

LITERACY RATE
99 percent (2009 estimate)

TIME LINE

IN CHILE	IN THE WORLD
7000–500 B.C. The Chinchorro settle near Arica; these hunter-gatherers mummify their dead in sand.	**753 B.C.** Rome is founded.
A.D. 200–300 The Mapuche people begin to develop; Diaguita culture flourishes.	**116–17 B.C.** The Roman Empire reaches its greatest extent, under Emperor Trajan (98-17b.c.).
1470–1535 The Incas invade Chile; their empire stretches 155 miles (250 km) south of Santiago.	**A.D. 600** Height of Mayan civilization
1520 Portuguese explorer Ferdinand Magellan's expedition passes through the Strait of Chile that now bears his name.	
1535 Spanish conquistador Diego de Almagro becomes the first European to set foot in Chile.	**1530** Beginning of transatlantic slave trade organized by Portuguese in Africa
1541 Pedro de Valdivia founds Santiago.	**1558–1603** Reign of Elizabeth I of England
1641 Mapuche Indians sign the Treaty of Quilín with the Spanish.	
1704 Alexander Selkirk is deserted on Robinson Crusoe Island for four years.	
1722 Easter Island is discovered on Easter Sunday by Jacob Roggeveen of Holland.	**1776** The U. S. Declaration of Independence
1810 Independence movements flourish throughout the Spanish colonies in America. First autonomous Chilean government is established.	**1789–1799** The French Revolution
1814 Spain retakes Chile.	
1817 Combined Chilean and Argentinean forces led by José de San Martín defeat Spanish troops.	
1818 Bernardo O'Higgins declares independence.	
1829–30 Civil war between the conservative landowners and the liberals, headed by President Ramón Freire.	
1830–60 Rule of "authoritarian" presidents.	**1861** The U.S. Civil War begins.
1879–83 War of the Pacific. Chile defeats the Peru-Bolivia confederation.	
1891 Chilean civil war over President José Manuel Balmaceda's policies of social reform.	**1914** World War I begins.

IN CHILE	IN THE WORLD

1925
President Arturo Alessandri grants the right to vote to literate males over age 21.

1939
World War II begins.

1945
Gabriela Mistral wins Nobel Prize in literature.

1949
Women gain the right to vote in national elections.

1949
The North Atlantic Treaty Organization (NATO) is formed.

1960
A catastrophic earthquake (9.5 Richter scale magnitude) and tsunami hit southern Chile.

1964
Eduardo Frei Montalva elected president and begins social reforms.

1966–1969
The Chinese Cultural Revolution

1970
Salvador Allende, a prominent socialist, is elected president.

1971
Pablo Neruda wins Nobel Prize in literature.

1973–89
A military coup overthrows President Allende. General Augusto Pinochet heads the military junta. Devastating human rights abuses characterize his dictatorship.

1986
Nuclear power disaster at Chernobyl in Ukraine

1988
A national plebiscite is held to determine if General Pinochet should continue to rule for another eight-year term. The "No" campaign triumphs and Pinochet steps down.

1990
Patricio Aylwin becomes the first democratically elected president since Allende.

1991
Breakup of Soviet Union

1997
Hong Kong is returned to China.

1998
While in England for medical treatment, General Pinochet is arrested for human rights crimes but eventually returns to Chile.

2000
Ricardo Lagos becomes the first socialist president since Allende.

2001
World population surpasses 6 billion.

2006
Dr. Michelle Bachelet becomes the first woman president. General Pinochet dies.

2009
Outbreak of flu virus H1N1 around the world

2010
Sebastian Piñera is the first right-wing president to be elected following the return to democracy. In February an earthquake measuring 8.8 on the Richter scale hits central Chile. In October 33 miners are all dramatically rescued after spending 70 days trapped in a mine near Copiapó.

2011
Twin earthquake and tsunami disasters strike northeast Japan, leaving 14,000 dead and thousands more missing.

GLOSSARY

animita (ah-nee-MEE-tah)
A small roadside shrine dedicated to a loved one who died at that spot, most likely in a traffic accident.

araucaria
Also called the monkey puzzle tree, this distinctive tree is considered by many to be the national tree of Chile.

Aymara
Indigenous group that lives in northern Chile, southern Peru, and Bolivia.

camanchaca (kah-mahn-CHAH-kah)
Extremely humid fog that rolls over the Andes from the ocean.

cartonero (kahr-toh-NEH-roh)
Someone who rides a bicycle through the streets at night and sorts through garbage for paper or cardboard to sell for recycling.

chueca (CHWAY-kah)
A game played by the Mapuche Indians, similar to field hockey.

Concertación
A political union of center and left-wing democratic parties.

criollos
The term used for pure Spaniards born on Spanish American soil during colonial times.

cueca (KWAY-kah)
Chile's national folk dance, featuring classic courtship attitudes.

empanada
A popular Chilean pastry stuffed with cheese, seafood, or meat, with chopped hard-cooked egg, raisins, and olives.

hacienda
A large farm or ranch. Also called *fundo* (FOON-doh).

huaso (WAH-soh)
A Chilean horseman or cowboy.

manta
A poncho worn by *huasos*.

Mapuche
Chile's largest indigenous group lives in southern Chile, primarily near the city of Temuco.

media luna (may-dee-ah LOO-nah)
In Spanish this means "half moon," and the stadium where a rodeo takes place is so named because of its shape.

moai (moh-ay)
A large stone sculpture, found on Easter Island, representing a head and torso.

once (OHN-say)
Chilean afternoon tea.

palafitos (pahl-ah-FEE-tohs)
Houses built on stilts at the water's edge to allow for high tides; they are found mainly on the island of Chiloé.

poblaciones callampas (poh-blah-see-OH-nehs kah-YAHM-pahs)
Low-income neighborhoods.

porotos granados (poh-ROH-tohs grah-NAH-doss)
A bean stew.

Restricción
A government policy to help reduce pollution in Santiago; between March and December cars without catalytic converters are prohibited from driving one day a week.

rucas (roo-KAHS)
The traditional simple homes of the Mapuche.

soroche (soh-ROH-chay)
Mountain or altitude sickness.

FOR FURTHER INFORMATION

BOOKS

Agosin, Marjorie. *Tapestries of Hope, Threads of Love: The Arpillera Movement in Chile,* 2nd ed. Lanham, MD: Rowman and Littlefield Publishers Inc., 2007.

DiPiazza, Francesca Davis. *Chile in Pictures.* Breckenridge, CO: Twenty-First Century Books, 2007.

Garcia Marquez, Gabriel. *Clandestine in Chile: The Adventures of Miguel Littin.* New York: New York Review Books: Classics, 2010.

Jani, Janak. *Chile Handbook.* 6th ed: Travel Guide to Chile. Bath, UK: Footprint Handbooks, 2010.

Ray, Leslie. *Language of the Land: The Mapuche in Argentina and Chile.* Copenhagen, Denmark: International Work Group for Indigenous Affairs, 2008.

Reifenberg, Steve. *Santiago's Children: What I Learned about Life at an Orphanage in Chile.* Austin, TX: University of Texas Press, 2008.

Roraff, Susan and Laura Camacho. *Culture Shock! Chile.* Singapore: Marshall Cavendish Editions, 2011.

Stadler, Hubert and Susanne Asal. *Chile: A Journey through Extremes.* Munich: Bucher Verlag, 2007.

WEBSITES

Chile Information Project, www.chip.cl/index

Lonely Planet: Chile, www.lonelyplanet.com/chile

Official travel guide to Chile, site of the National Tourism Board. www.chile.travel/

Official website of Chile: This Is Chile, www.thisischile.cl

Santiago Times newspaper, www.santiagotimes.cl

World Travel Guide: Chile, www.worldtravelguide.net/chile

FILMS/DVDS

Nostalgia for the Light, Icarus Films, 2010.

Easter Island Underworld, National Geographic, 2010.

The Battle of Chile, Icarus Films, 2009.

The Maid (La Nana), Elephant Eye Films, 2009.

Pinochet's Last Stand, HBO Home Video, 2008.

History—Digging for the Truth: Giants of Easter Island, A&E Television Entertainment, 2008.

Michael Palin: Full Circle, BBC Warner, 2008.

Machuca, Passion River Studios, 2007.

Soccer Stories (*Historias de Fútbol*), Terra Entertainment, 2006.

BIBLIOGRAPHY

BOOKS

Box, Ben (ed.). *South American Handbook 2001.* 87th ed. Chicago: Passport Books, 2000.

Brosse, Jacques. *Great Voyages of Discovery: Circumnavigators and Scientists 1764—1843,* (translated by Stanley Hochman). New York: Facts on File Publications, 1983.

Center for Public Policy Analysis. *Informe País: Estado del Medio Ambiente en Chile 1999.* Santiag University of Chile, 1999.

Constable, Pamela and Arturo Valenzuela. *A Nation of Enemies: Chile under Pinochet.* New York: W.W. Norton, 1993.

Devine, Elizabeth and Nancy L. Braganti. *The Traveler's Guide to Latin American Customs and Manners.* New York: St. Martin's Press, 2000.

Elacqua, Gregory, Dante Contreras and Felipe Salazar. *Scaling Up in Chile.* Vol. 8, No. 3. Cambridge, MA: EducationNext, 2008.

Joelson, Daniel. *Chilenismos: A Dictionary and Phrasebook for Chilean Spanish.* New York: Hippocrene Books, 2005.

————. *Tasting Chile: A Celebration of Authentic Chilean Foods and Wines.* New York: Hippocrene Books, 2004.

WEBSITES

American Chamber of Commerce in Chile, www.amchamchile.cl

Banco Central de Chile: New Statistics Database, www.bcentral.cl

Biodiversidad en Chile, www.conama.cl

Business Chile Magazine, www.businesschile.cl

Central Bank of Chile, www.bcentral.cl/eng

Central Intelligence Agency, The World Factbook: Chile, https://www.cia.gov/library/publications/the-world-factbook/index.html

Economy Watch: Country Economic Profiles, Chile Economic Structure, www.economywatch.co

Education Next, www.educationnext.org

Exploring the Universe from Chile, www.businesschile.cl

Food and Agriculture Organization of the United Nations: Country Briefs, Chile: Agricultural Sector, www.fao.org

Inter-American Development Bank: Countries, Chile: Indicators, www.iadb.org

International Monetary Fund: Country Info: Chile and the IMF, IMF Executive Board Concludes 2010 Article IV Consultation with Chile, www.imf.org

La Corporación Nacional Forestal: Control Desertificación, www.conaf.cl

World Bank: Chile Country Brief, www.worldbank.org

INDEX

INDEX